Caernarfon Sail, 1814

1. Left foreground – sloop:- rail bulwark, fixed bowsprit, running squaresail yard a-cockbill
2. Right foreground – sloop:- two headsails, gaff mainsail loose footed, gaff topsail, bulwark rail
3. Right background – two masted topsail schooner
4. Left background – two masted ketch, two headsails, two squaresails on main mast
5. Centre foreground – small ketch rigged fishing boat, mainsail loose footed, mizen fore & aft spritsail with outrigger (or could be GIG boat).

(National Library of Wales)

Caernarfonshire Sail

Owen F. G. Kilgour

First published in 2008

Cover photograph: *Vilma*, built 1934 at the Bronsodde shipyard Denmark,
as a ketch rigged fishing vessel.
Gross tonnage: 20.05; length 47ft (17.4m); beam 14.6ft (4.5m); draft 6.6ft (2.03m).
Construction: 2 inch oak planking on 5 inch oak frames.
Employed as a fishing vessel for sixty two years.
Sold 1996 to Scott Metcalfe, Waterfront Marine boatyard, Porth Penrhyn.
Underwent total restoration and reconstruction into a single topsail schooner.
Launched during 2000 as the first wooden topsail schooner to be produced in
Caernarfonshire for over seventy five years, since the launch of the schooner *Gestiana*
in Porthmadog in 1913.
Present owner Scott Metcalfe, Waterfront Marine boatyard, Porth Penrhyn.

ISBN: 978-184524-107-0

Published by
Gwasg Carreg Gwalch,
12 Iard yr Orsaf, Llanrwst, Wales, LL26 0EH.
Tel: 01492 642031 Fax: 01492 641502
e-mail: llyfrau@carreg-gwalch.com
www. carreg-gwalch.com

Printed and published in Wales.

DEDICATION

In memory of Captain Robert Hugh Jones,
Groeshigol, Trefor, Caernarfonshire,
and all seafarers who have no known resting place,
memorial or commemoration, other than the sea.

SCHOONERMEN

Great in this,
They made small ships do
Big things, leaping hurdles
Of the stiff sea, horse against horses
In the tide race.
                  What has Rio
To do with Pwllheli? Ask winds
Bitter for ever
With their black shag. Ask the quays
Stained with spittle.
                  Four days out
With bad cargo
Fever took the crew;
The mate and boatswain
Peering in turn
Through the sprays window,
Brought her home. Memory aches
In the bones rigging. If tales were tall
Waves were taller.
                  From long years
In a salt school, caned by brine,
They came landward
With eyes of boys,
The Welsh accent
Thick in their sails.

R.S.Thomas (1913- 2000)

CONTENTS

ACKNOWLEDGEMENTS

I appreciate with thanks the help given by Dr Ronald Hope of the Seafarers Education Service during all my years as a writer.

To Geraint Owen and Mark Craven for their computer assistance in preparing the typescript.

I also thank a shipmate and good friend over many years; Bosun J. Glyn Jones, for much technical advice.

I am indebted to Myrddin ap Dafydd at Gwasg Carreg Gwalch for his ready and continual support for this proposal.

I express my sincere gratitude and appreciation to Christopher Rudd, a friend for almost thirty years during my relationship with the Jubilee Sailing Trust as honorary regional organiser north Wales, and in particular for his inspired establishment of offshore sailing for so many people, able bodied and disabled in Britain.

Throughout the work I have drawn heavily on the first hand diverse maritime experiences, gained through a long friendship with the late Bertie and Percy Japheth of Trefor, whose eminent ship modelling, artwork and shipwright skills, remain as an abiding influence for me and so many others.

I have also enjoyed the pleasure of seeing traditional wooden boatbuilding skills underway at two boat building yards in Caernarfonshire; *Classical Sailboats* at Wern Difyr, Bethel, and the *Waterfront Marine* at Port Penrhyn. Here traditional shipwright skills flourish in the construction and rebuilding of wooden boats, from clinker rowing boats, through carvel hulled nobbies to topsail schooners, together with their masting and rigging. Caernarfonshire maritime heritage is indebted to the proprietors John Jones, Andy Long and Scott Metcalfe who continue to promote and maintain the valued skills of wooden boatbuilding.

I also value the kindness of Scott in reading and checking the technical content of the proof copy.

I also cherish the memories of my companionship ashore

and afloat with the late Aled Eames and late Frank Rhys Jones, distinguished maritime historians, who together widened my horizon concerning the maritime heritage of Caernarfonshire and shared in my hopes for a sail training ship for Wales, both kindly encouraged me as a maritime scientist, and together they inspired what I have attempted to do.

No single person other than Mici Plwm has done so much to actively nurture the idea of a sailing training ship for Wales by his active participation of JST voyages from Wales.

* * *

Note: The sources of plate illustration material are indicated in each illustration caption.

I am very grateful to the Gwynedd Archives Service allowing me generous usage of the material from the collections in their care. Also to Llyfrgell Genedlaethol Cymru; Christopher Rudd; Gwilym Jones; The Sail Training Association of Western Australia; Ceredigion Museum Aberystwyth; The Spirit of Adventure Trust New Zealand; Jubilee Sailing Trust; and The HM Bark Endeavour Foundation Pty.

I thank for the right to reproduce *Schoonermen* by R. S. Thomas.

Also: Mike Arridge, Andy Long, and Scott Metcalfe for permission to reproduce their photographic material.

If the publishers and the author have inadvertently overlooked any providers of illustration material, or other material, we will be pleased to make the necessary amendments at the first opportunity.

INTRODUCTION

The main sources for this book, for which I am greatly indebted, are the valuable and informative books, which provide a comprehensive coverage of the Maritime History of Caernarfonshire, written by the pioneer Welsh maritime historian, David Thomas; author of *Hen Longau a Longwyr Cymru*, Cardiff 1949 and *Hen Longau Sir Gaernarfon, (HLSG)* Caernarfon 1952 and Gwasg Carreg Gwalch 2007.

I have undertaken a general analysis of the Appendixes One and Two from the latter book, and used the outcome as the basis of identification of sailing vessel types and their evolution in Caernarfonshire from earliest times to 1913.

The identification of any object, or thing, depends on the visual recognition of salient characteristics of the materials, body form, or body structure. In the same way the rig of a wooden sailing vessel is identified on the basis of its individual body form comprising the; hull, masting rigging and sails.

The different types of sailing vessels have been given common names, many of which have lost their specific meaning through time, and the vessels are now extinct with little if any physical evidence remaining of them.

The names of the vessel types mentioned in *Hen Longau Sir Gaernarfon* are presented in this book, and each type described giving its main known structural characteristics, with reference to the average vessel dimensions, hull composition, masting, runnning and standing rigging and sails; features which identify the type of vessel in a systematic way, and hopefully a way which may capture the interest of a generation seeking knowledge of their past maritime heritage; in addition it will be of value to the period ship modeller.

Structural and other maritime terms are written in italics when they appear for the first time in the text. Alternative spellings, or names for terms are also provided.

The evolution of the wooden sailing vessel is presented as being a process of gradual change in vessel body structure, taking place under human influence throughout past centuries; a process which has seen the extinction of certain vessel types, followed by survival of other sailing vessel types being better adapted to the environmental and economic factors of their time.

Evolution is a continuous process; I consider the present state of sailing vessel evolution is in a state of dormancy enabling its survival and emergence when future environmental conditions favour it, as a renewed carbon-free, and efficient means of water transport.

Finally I have taken this opportunity to make a plea for a sail training vessel for Wales in keeping with other maritime nations worldwide, and trust it will succeed.

Fred Kilgour
Old Colwyn
2008

1. EARLY WATERCRAFT

During the Middle Stone Age (BC8500) the people of North Wales lived in the coastal areas, now completely submerged under the sea which has risen since that time. The daily weather forecast would have been "continuing warm and dry" making the sea warm and attractive to gather shellfish in the sand or rock pools, or to swim and experience the sensation of being afloat. Many of these early coastal dwellers exercised their ingenuity by finding ways of keeping afloat and extending their fishing range into deeper water. In time they developed *watercraft* also collectively called *vessels* as the means to transport themselves on lakes and seas.

Without heavy cutting tools, axes or adzes, the early watercraft builders had to use what was freely to hand littering the beaches as tree trunks, the bloated bodies of drowned animals such as deer, feral cattle and pigs, and timber from the nearby woodlands of birch, willow, hazel, oak, elm, alder, pine and juniper.

Single Logs would provide buoyancy and support to keep a person afloat aided by paddling for propulsion or to change direction.

Log Rafts made by lashing several logs together using slender flexible tree roots or saplings, provided a platform that could be raised further out of the water on bloated animal bodies, or inflated deer skins; propulsion would have been by hand paddling or flat paddles. The oldest known wooden paddles date from around BC7500, and were found in Yorkshire.

Raft vessels as a means of transport continues to the present day-made from papyrus reeds, or bamboo.

Bark Canoes built with bark stripped from birch trees can be formed into a shell-like canoe shape and its ends sewn together with sinews or flexible roots. The lengthwise, or *fore and aft*, strengthening is achieved by means of hazel twigs arranged on the upper sides of the canoe, whilst stronger hazel branches fitted transversely or *athwart* provides

beamlike strengthening for *thwarts*, seats, for oarsmen to paddle the vessel.
Bark canoes continue to the present day, and the canoe constructed from different materials is a popular sporting vessel.

Skin Vessels would be constructed during the Middle Stone Age from deer hide, tanned with birch bark, stretched over a skeleton framework of hazel, or willow branches- deer bone could also be used, which also found usage for making fishing harpoons. This method of construction was used in making baskets, tents, and dome shaped huts the people lived in.

Coracles are bowl shaped vessels and are still in use in many place in the world – Wales, Ireland, England and also in Oamaru, New Zealand, where they feature in an annual coracle building festival.

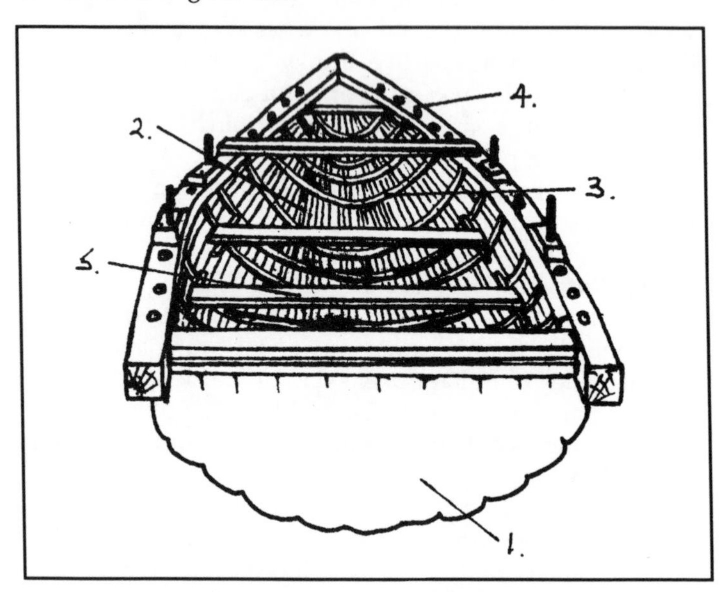

Figure 1. The curragh or Celtic skin boat.

Curraghs Figure 1, are Irish vessels which have a structural plan that has survived from antiquity, they are elongated vessels in a fore and aft structure. They are in continuous usage in the West of Ireland.

• The *skin* (1) of tanned and greased cowhide, or linen, cotton or canvas coated with tar, is stretched and sewn over a skeleton framework of willow, elm, alder, ash or hazel branches arranged longitudinally as *stringers* (2), and transversely as *ribs* (3) fixed into longitudinal *gunwales* (4) as shown in Figure 1.

• Dimensions of a large curragh average 18ft (6m) length, 3ft (1m) breadth and 2ft 6in (0.8m) depth and weighs about 120lb – 60kg

• Propulsion is mainly by means of four oars upto 14ft (4.3m) in length, a small sail, either a *lugsail* or *squaresail,* can be fitted. The *thwarts* (5) provide transverse strengthening, and upto 8 people can be carried.

• Usage is mainly as people and animal carriers, fishing and upto half a ton of granite setts could be carried as cargo.

Skin boats were in use from BC500 to 300AD and voyages were being made well into the North Atlantic reaching Iceland and Greenland with regular crossings across the Irish sea.

Kayaks and umiaks are still in use in North America and Greenland.

Dugouts were vessels made about BC4000-2000, during the New Stone Age, by hollowing out tree trunks using stone axes, adzes or fire, to produce a shell-like structure. This period had a climate that was warm and wet, and the people were occupied in farming, instead of hunting.

Heavy stone tools were available from the Graig Lwyd stone tool factory above Penmaenmawr producing stone axes, adzes, hammers, and chisels; evidently much of the product reached various parts of Britain possibly transported in skin vessels. Lighter stone tools, awls, scrapers, knives, axes and adzes were produced at Mynydd Rhiw in Llŷn.

The remains of dugouts have been found all over Wales and seemingly were used in sheltered waters of lakes and bays, various types of dugout were produced by joining two or more lengthwise – or splitting into two halves and rejoining the halves together via a bridging piece.

Plank Built Vessels, Figure 2, were the result of the discovery that tree trunks could be split into *planks* using stone axes or wedges-later these planks could be shaped by adzing.

Evidence for the existence of plank built vessels were found at North Ferriby near Hull in 1937, and the remains were radiocarbon dated to the Bronze Age BC1500. Radiocarbon dating is a method used to estimate the age of organic remains of plants and animals including wood which are all biodegradable and consequently little remains of wooden watercraft of antiquity.

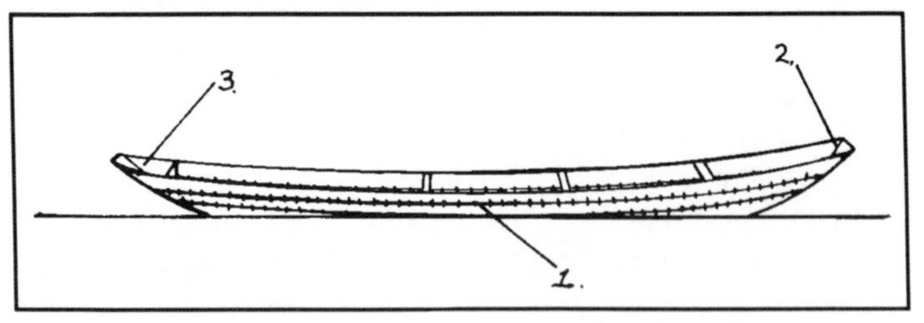

Figure 2. The North Ferriby planked-up boat.

The Ferriby planked vessel, Figure 2, had the following features;

- Dimensions approximately 52ft (16m) in length and 8.5ft (2.6m) breadth overall. This indicates a very large open vessel almost 3.5 times longer than a curragh, and larger than the average smack or sloop to be built 3000 years later, thus indicating the potential of building large vessels from wooden planks.
- Hull is constructed from nine oak planks obtained by splitting logs down the centre; three on the flat bottom as *keel planks*, and three each side (1). The planks are *laid* or placed edge to edge, and *fastened* together by means of stitching with tough flexible thin branches of yew. Cross beams of ash strengthen the bottom of the hull, the beams being held in position by means of cleats which had been adzed or cut into the plank surface. The hull is made watertight by filling the seams with a *caulking* of twisted moss strands covered with flat wood strips held down by the stitching.
- The completed hull resembles an elongated punt, with an upturned short *bow* (2) and a *stern* with a small platform (3).

• The vessel appears to be a ferry and could carry an estimated four tons of cargo. Propulsion was likely by poling or by paddles and maybe a light sail was set.

In 1991 the remains of a similar Bronze Age boat were found in Dover, it appears to have been a seagoing vessel able to cross the channel to Europe.

Vessels similar to these planked vessels must have eventually been built in Caernarfonshire in order to carry heavy cargo along the coast.

These earliest types of vessels are still to be found in many parts of the world today, each adapted to its environment and supply of resources, and providing a basic form of water transport, suited to a simple way of life.

During the next 3000 years, human beings being innovative, will make changes to their watercraft and continue this change in a process of *evolution,* producing more efficient watercraft able to travel to the horizon which they could see from the shore, to return and then make distant voyages to distant parts of the Earth. This evolutionary process will be traced in future chapters over its long time scale, emphasis will be made on the change in vessel *form* and how these structural changes produce distinct kinds of vessels with clearly recognisable structural features which *identify* the *type* of craft. Generally the smaller vessels will be called *boats* and the larger vessels will be called *ships.*

Throughout the book the general term *rig* will be used to cover the structural and functional features of a vessel namely the *hull, masting, rigging and sails,* all of which identify the vessel *type,* such as *cog, caravel, brig, barque* etc.

2. EARLY PLANKBUILT VESSELS

From the time the earliest planked vessels existed at Ferriby, new types of vessels appeared gradually, developing a structure built up of many planks fastened together to make an outer watertight covering forming the vessel body or *hull*. The hull frequently had a planked *deck* which enclosed a cavity of the *hold*.

During the next 1500 years the hull of new types of vessels would undergo change in its form or shape mainly by *laying* and *fastening* the planks in different ways.

Three plankbuilt wooden cargo vessels for the period BC50 to 400AD will be considered from Brittany, Britain and Italy respectively.

Celtic Plankbuilt Vessel

The Veneti were seafaring Celtic people living in Brittany, and in Cornwall. It is thought the Veneti had relationships with Gwynedd, known by its Latin name of Venedotia.

During the Iron Age, BC800 to 43AD, the people inhabited the coastal headlands, which protected them from seaward attack through the tidal movements, making their strongholds into islands at high tides, and were protected by stretches of perilous rocky shores at low tides.

The Veneti had a large fleet of vessels which confronted the naval fleet of Julius Caesar who provided the only known description of the Veneti vessels:

- The single decked hull was composed of many thick oak planks forming high sides to the vessel. The bottom planking may have been fastened to *cross beams* with iron bolts. Seaweed may have been used to caulk the seams. The flat bottomed hull was ideal for taking the ground at low tide, it also kept the vessel upright due to the low *deadrise* of the hull. The flat bottomed hull is a feature of Celtic built boats that will be seen in future centuries.
- Sail was a leather squaresail bent to a *yard* crossed on the single mast.
- Steering was by means of one or two steering oars.

• The strongly built vessel with its rough surfaced hull could weather mighty seas experienced in the Bay of Biscay and the Irish sea. We can only guess that these vessels visited the shores of northern Wales bringing trade and migrating people from Brittany, Spain and Portugal.

British Plankbuilt Vessel

The remains of a British built vessel, dated as about 150AD to 200AD, were found on a bank of the River Thames at Blackfriars, near to today's St Paul's Cathedral.

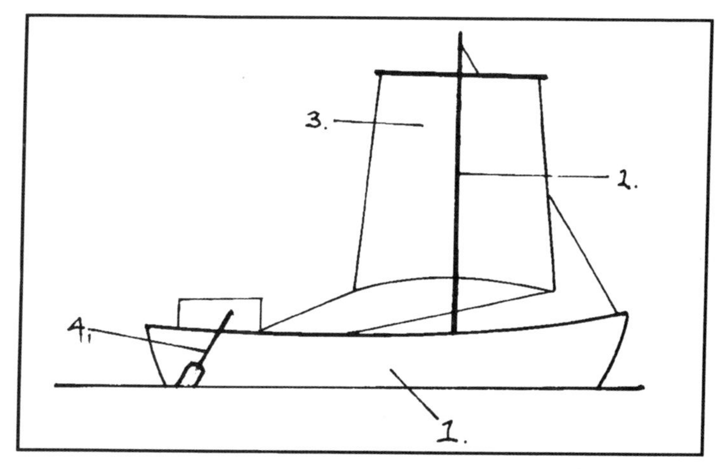

Figure 3. The Blackfriars barge.

Figure 3 shows the hypothetical reconstruction which indicates a heavily built seagoing bargelike vessel. The characteristic features of this type of vessel are summarised:

• Dimensions; 55ft (17m) length x 22ft (6.75m) breadth x 7ft (2.2m) depth. The vessel was round and beamy, with a straight stem and bluff bows

The hull (1) *planking* was of oak 2 to 3 inches thick, fastened to *timbers, or ribs,* by means of iron nails, upto 27 inches long, driven through previously inserted wooden *treenails,* the emerging iron nails were *clenched* over into the timber face (see Figure 5).

• The hull bottom was flat, a feature of Celtic built

vessels, with an advantage to take the ground at low water leaving the vessel upright.

- Caulking in the seams was composed of hazel twigs.
- A single mast (2) supported a woven material squaresail (3) and two steering oars (4) directed the vessels movement.
- The planked deck had a *cargo hatch* and small *deckhouse* aft.

The remains of a very similar constructed smaller vessel were found in 1993 at Magor, Gwent, having dimensions of 37ft (11.35m) length x 10.3ft (3.2m) breadth and 2.93ft (0.9m) depth and could carry an estimated cargo of upto 6.5 tonnes, driven with a *lugsail* on a single mast.

This is the oldest open, undecked, wooden sailing vessel discovered in Wales and is dated to the late third century AD. One can assume that many similar handy sized coasting vessels of this type worked in Caernarfonshire for many centuries.

Roman Plankbuilt Vessel

The Roman invasion of Snowdonia happened in 61AD. The invaders must have been impressed by the Veneti type heavily constructed, highsided and flat bottomed, plankbuilt

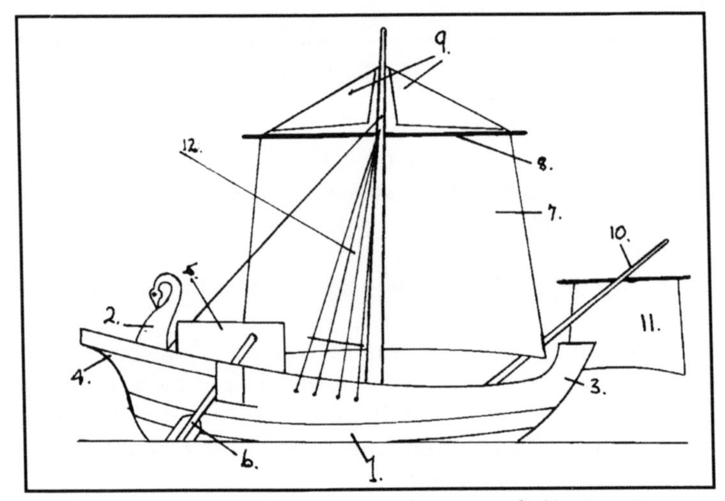

Figure 4. Roman merchant vessel rig.

vessels to be seen along the northern Wales coast and must have abandonded any hopes of ramming these sturdy vessels by means of their warships. Equally impressed were the local inhabitants by the graceful, fine lined, smooth hulled, Roman cargo vessels sailing with stores to the forts at Caernarfon, Caerhun and the naval coastguard fort at Caergybi.

Scenes engraved in shallow stone carvings, or bas-relief, found in the port of Rome, namely Ostia, and dated 150-250AD, show a typical medium sized Roman cargo vessel, Figure 4.

The following are some of the main structural characteristics of this type of plankbuilt vessel, specifically called a *corbita,* shown in Figure 4.

• Dimensions; 75ft (23m) length x 19.5ft (5.9m) breadth. Estimated cargo tonnage 86 tonnes.

Much larger corbita type ships were also known of 180ft (55m) length, 45ft (14m) breadth and 44ft (13.5m) depth – ships in the proper meaning of the term, that is large vessels which could carry small boats.

• The hull had a broad rounded shape, the two layers of planks -inner and outer- were laid flush, edge to edge, and fastened by means of mortice and tenon joints. The planking commenced at the keel, to produce a smooth *carvel* built hull, see Plate 7.

• *Wales* (1) were bolted lengthwise along the hull from the waterline, to act as protective rubbing strakes, when the vessel was berthed alongside the stone quay walls in the Mediterranean port harbours. On grounding, the round bottomed hull with its deadrise would cause the vessel to lie on its side.

• The *stern* (2) was curved ending in a carved swan head and neck; the *stem* (3) was also curved but not ornately carved.

• Strong transverse beams supported a single *deck* which extended aft as a overhanging *poop deck* (4). A deckhouse (5) had a roof which served as navigation deck and was close to the two large hoistable steering oars (6).

• The mainmast had a large square *mainsail* (7) bent to a *yard* (8), in addition there were two triangular topsails or *raffees* (9). The foremast, or *artemon* mast (10), was steeply sloping and was stepped, like the main mast, into the keelson, it carried a single artemon squaresail (11) bent to a yard.

The *rigging* (12), standing and running, appeared more complex and was well made in comparison to the Celtic vessels.

The Roman cargo vessel would have been the swan amongst the Caernarfon ducks! The vessel was a typical product of the Roman Empire reflecting the skills of its woodworkers and shipbuilders, working in one of the most civilised developed countries in the world during the period BC27 to 476AD – something that would not be seen in Britain until the formation of the British Empire – some 1200 years later on.

Cymru a'r Môr articles relating to early plankbuilt vessels include; "A Romano-british boat recovered from a site in Gwent", Owain T. Roberts and Sean McGrail, Vol 23, 2002.

3. SCANDINAVIAN CLINKER BUILT VESSELS

Scandinavian people living in the maritime countries of Norway, Sweden and parts of Denmark, were engaged in seafaring and agricultural activities. From about BC300 they produced a unique class of plank built vessels collectively known as the Scandinavian *clincher (clinker)* built vessels.

The terms clinker, clincher, clencher are synonymous for clench built vessel hulls in Britain and used generally in contrast to the American term, lapstrake. Clinker is the preferred shipwrights term in use currently and throughout the 20th century. Clincher and clencher, are the earlier *historical* terms.

Clinker is derived from the method of *fastening* the strakes, whereas as lapstrake is derived from the method of *laying* the strakes.

The process of development of these clincher built vessels occupied a period of about 1300 years to 1000AD during which a variety of vessels ranging from small fishing boats to

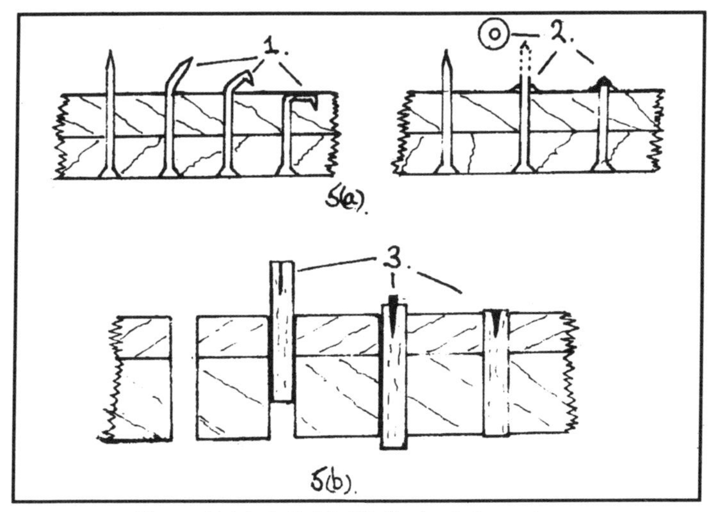

Figure 5 (a) & 5 (b). Hull plank fastenings.

large warships, or longships, were built, which shared the following general characteristics of the class;

• The *clincher* built hull is an elongated, round bottomed form. The pine or oak planks are broad and thin and are *laid* partly overlapping at the edges and *fastened* by metal nails or wooden treenails, driven through the overlapping planks, see Plate 36. Figure 5 (a) shows how the nails are *fastened* after being driven through through the wood and the emerging nail end is turned and the point *clenched* into the plank surface (1). Alternatively the nail is riveted through a *rove* (2).

Figure 5 (b) shows how the *treenails,* or cylinders of wood, were driven through previously bored holes and a small treenail *wedge* fixed in the open end (3) to secure the fastening.

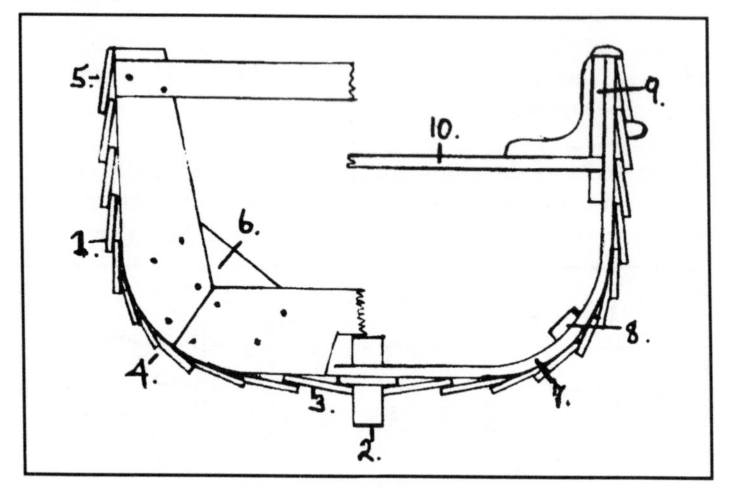

Figure 6. Clincher hull midsection structure.

• Figure 6 shows a sectional view of a clincher built rowing boat, Plate 36, and how the *strakes* (1) overlap one another to form a *shell structure.* The first strake is laid close to the *keel* (2) and is called the *garboard strake* (3). The laying and fastening continues through the turn of the *bilge* (4) until it reaches the highest strake called the *sheerstrake* (5). During this construction a *mould* (6) is in place to help shape the hull and is removed once the *shell* has been completed.

• A strengthening framework is fitted inside the completed shell consisting of *timbers* or ribs (7) arranged transversely. Longitudinally arranged stringers (8) and gunwales (9) are then fitted together with transverse thwarts (10).

• The hull is *double ended* or pointed at each end, see Figure 7. A high curving, or straight, *stempost* connects with the *forward end* of the keel and a curving, or straight, *sternpost* connects with the keel at the *after end*. The ends are sharp and serve to cut the water.

• The completed hulls are lightweight and transportable overland.

• The shallow *draught* allows the vessel to float in shallow water.

• The hull has remarkable flexibility and this is used to advantage by absorbing and transmitting the wave energy throughout the hull and preventing the hull from breaking up in rough seas, as would occur with a rigid structure.

Steering is by means of a single *steerboard* oar mounted on the starboard side (right looking forward).

The Scandinavian vessels were fast under oar or sail and capable of 10 to 15 knots in favourable conditions.

Saxon or Previking Period

This period extended from BC300 to 600AD and included the time of the departure of the Romans from Wales and the invasion of Britain by Saxon or Germanic people during the 430sAD.

The Scandinavian vessels constructed during this period were mainly with oars and *without* mast or sail. One variety of Scandinavian vessel (Nydam) brought the Saxons to Britain, they had acquired skills to build this boat from their Viking neighbours.

Viking Period

This period extended from 600 to 1066AD, during this time the Saxon had established their rule in Britain, but the country was subject to Viking raids, and Wales experienced the first Viking raids in 852AD continuing until about 1000AD. These raids took place over 150 years when the

Viking seaborne warriors raided and pillaged monasteries and churches for silver and gold and took slaves, which were transported as a compact cargo in their warships. Viking trading centres were established in Anglesey, on the Ormes, Dublin, the Isle of Man and in south Wales.

The success of the Viking incursion into Britain, Greenland, Iceland, Faeroes, North America, the Baltic and European countries was entirely due to their shipbuilding skills which were continually undergoing development into a variety of vessels within the class; these included warships or longships upto 75ft (23m) in length; fishing boats upto 21ft (6.5m) in length; and cargo ships upto 75ft (23m) in length. The vessels were propelled partly by oars, some had a *hoistable* mast and squaresail, others had a permanent mast and squaresail.

Some of these vessels are to be seen in the Bayeux tapestry showing the Normans in longboats, Plate 34, the Normans originated from Scandinavia and settled in France bringing their boatbuilding skills with them.

No doubt Caernarfonshire people were impressed with the Scandinavian clincher hull and soon copied the method of construction when they eventually built their own wooden clincher boats using local resources, without plans, and by rule of thumb, on any available piece of land, this has continued until the present day. Later the clincher hull form has been replicated in glass reinforced plastic GRP.

Thee Knarr or Knorr

The most famous of the Scandinavian clincher built vessels was the *knarr* or *knorr*, a cargo carrier also an ocean going vessel shown in Figure 7. This vessel was used in voyages of discovery to Britain and across the Atlantic and would have been the type of vessel familiar to Caernarfonshire people – in fact Edward I had vessels built somewhat similar to the knarr to patrol the Menai Strait.

The following summarises the knarr's main characteristics;

- Dimensions; 54ft (16.5m) length x 13ft (4m) breadth x 6ft (1.8m) depth. These dimensions indicate the hull is beamy and deep.

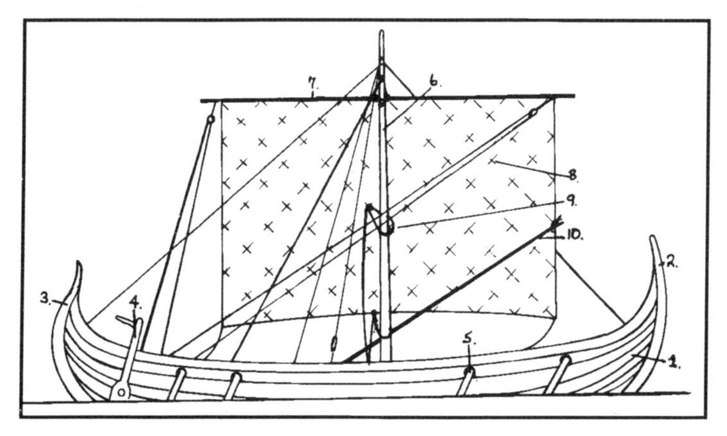

Figure 7. Scandinavian knarr rig.

- Cargo carried upto 10 tons and 30 people.
- The hull was built up of 8 to 12 strakes (1) of pine each side of the keel, to produce a relatively highsided vessel. The hull bottom was rounded, producing a *deadrise* causing the hull to lie on its bilge sides when the vessel was taking the ground.
- The stem (2) was either curved or straight, and the bows were bluff resembling a female bust – this feature survived into the female figurehead bust seen in vessels of the 1800s. See page 174.
- The stern (3) was either curved or straight, and like the stem provided a *cutwater,* allowing the vessel to go astern without having to turn in its full length.
- There were two small decks in the bow and stern.
- A *steerboard* (4) was connected to the starboard stern quarter.
- Four pairs of oars (5) – used mainly for harbour manouvering.
- The mast was a single, one piece pole, permanently stepped mast (6) crossed by a yard (7) supporting a *squaresail* made of woven material wool or linen, diagonally strengthened with a lattice arrangement of leather strips (8). A band of rope the *parrel or parrall* (9) held the middle and lower edge of the sail, and another rope held the yard to the mast. A reaching spar, or *beitass* (10) was used to hold the sail

edge outwards when under way.

- The rigging was made of walrus hide.
- An iron anchor and iron chain together with a *windlass* to hoist the sail and anchor completed the deck fittings.

Norman or Postviking Period

This period was from 1066AD until about 1400AD, included the conquest of Britain by the Normans and the expulsion of the Vikings. During this time the Cinque Ports of Dover, Hastings, Sandwich, Romney and Hythe were developed as naval stations each of which had a fleet of vessels similar to the knarr, proof of the Scandinavian clincher vessels excellence as a warship and good shipbuilding technique now adopted in Norman Britain.

The main feature of the Cinque Port vessel was the presence of *castles* fitted to the heads of the stern, stem and the mast, and called *sterncastle, forecastle-focsle* and *topcastle* respectively. These castles were fighting platforms for soldiers.

In adddition to having the knarr's basic structure, the Cinque Port warships had sails with two or three rows of *reef points* as a means to shorten the sail in heavy weather.

These vessels, apart from local defence, were used to carry the Crusaders together with their horses to the Mediterranean.

Ultimately the Scandinavian class vessel became restricted in its usage by its small cargo capacity, with developing trade calling for bigger cargo vessels. Also large clincher built vessels of over 100 ft (30.7m) in length were found to be unstable in rough weather and they ultimately became obsolete towards the middle 1300sAD.

Survival

The clincher or lapstrake built hull has survived over 2000 years to the present day, and its popularity continues in rowing boats and sailing boats.

Boats are found today in the Shetland Isles with very strong characteristics of the Scandinavian type vessel, and are called "fourerns" with four oars and "sixerns" for the large boat with six oars, both have a single lugsail, are clinker built and double-ended; see Plate 35.

Plate 36 shows a typical example of these lovely boats built in Gwynedd at the Classic Sailboat yard at Bethel where the traditional building methods are still used, with the sitka spruce planks fastened with bronze and copper nails to elm ribs together with an oak keel. Iroko wood is used for the thwarts, sheer plank and transom. The transom is a later development from the double ended Viking type vessel.

4. THE COG

David Thomas lists vessels of the 14th and 15th centuries in his Appendix 1 of *HLSG*, and other records for the 12th and 14th centuries refer to different kinds of sailing vessels, one referred to in this period is the *cog*. In addition the individual vessels, in many cases, are given names as for example; the cog *Sanctie Marie*, 1308, of Conwy, the cog *St Mary*, 1350, of Tenby, and the cog *Le Kateryne*, 1370, Beaumaris. The names are mainly feminine, possibly a sign of admiration for the vessels beauty and sailing grace which continues to the present time.

The term cog is used to name and identify a *type* of sailing vessel and to distinguish it from other types of vessel of the same period in other parts of Britain-such names as *hulk, balinger, picard, crayer* and *buss* appear in records. The cog is frequently mentioned in Welsh literature during the period 1350AD to 1450AD as a cargo carrier capable of carrying cargoes of betwen 4 to 40 tun – very much more than the old Celtic and Scandinavian vessels. The cog would have been familiar to people at the ports of Caernarfon, Pwllheli, Porth Dinllaen, Bangor, and Conwy.

Elsewhere in north Germany the cog was very much evident in the literature from 1200AD and coexisted with the Scandinavian class vessels, it appears to have undergone gradual development and became the main factor in contributing to the wealth of North German and nearby countries, who were united in a trading union called the Hanseatic League. The new towns developing within the league used the image of the cog in their *town seals*, because the vessel was the main carrier in the powerful Hanseatic shipping line, a role it maintained for over 200 years until the 1400sAD, trading to the Baltic, Britain and the Mediterranean.

Cog Construction

The remains of an almost complete cog were excavated from the harbour at Bremen in 1962. The investigations showed

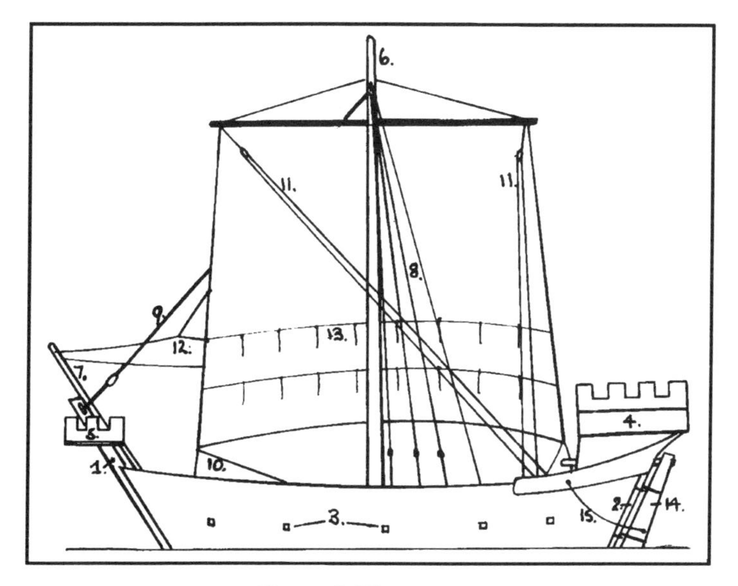

Figure 8. The cog rig.

the vessel was dated to 1380 and had been undergoing construction and was swept away from the *stocks*, and sunk into the harbour mud. The vessel, Figure 8, had the following characteristics:

• Dimensions; 77ft (23.6m) length x 24ft (7.4m) breadth. The draught was 10ft (3.1m); meaning that depth of water for the vessel to float.

• Hull appears heavily built in clincher style, and had sharp pointed ends together with straight inclined stem (1) and stern posts (2) to which the ends of the oak strakes were fixed.

• Bottom was flat, a typical Celtic feature allowing the vessel to remain upright when taking the ground, and composed of four strakes each side laid flush edge to edge and fixed by means of treenails into the timber, or *floor*, framework. In later cogs the bottom is reduced to a single *keel plank*.

• Sides are high and straight, composed of over 8 strakes from above the bilge. The planks are laid in clincher fashion with edges overlapping and fastened with clenched iron nails together with treenails fastened into the rib framework. A caulking of moss laid in a groove together with a batten along the lap edge seals the hull shell.

• A *ceiling* makes up the hold lining of planks, laid edge to edge, and fixed to the framework inside the hold. This is a feature of cargo carriers and functions to protect the hull from damage from the cargo.

• A single deck, called the *upper deck*, extends the vessel length and is laid on *transverse beams* (3) the ends of which protrude through the vessels sides. A vessel is said to be on its *beam ends* when it heels over or lies on its side and may capsize. Hatches or removable panels give access to the hold. The earlier smaller cogs were undecked as open vessels.

• *Castles;* fore. stern and top, were the fighting platforms in warship cogs. In merchant cogs the after or stern castle (4) blended as a permanent structure and functioned as a *quarter-deck*, whilst the forecastle *(focsle)* (5) was reduced. A small deckhouse may have been provided aft.

• Masting consisted of a single pole see Plate 22 main mast (6) stepped into the keelson, and a *bowsprit* – boltsprit (7).

• The sail, supported on a yard, was a single squaresail made of woven hemp canvas. Hemp was also used to make the *standing* rigging which supported the mast by means of rigging *shrouds* (8) and a *forestay* (9). The *running* rigging which moved the sail and yard included the sheets, tack (10) and braces (11). *Bowlines* (12) connected to the sails vertical edge were led to the bowspirit (7) at the bow.

The squaresail was shortened by means of two rows of *reef bands* and their attached *reef lines* (13)

• Rudder (14) was hung on the stern post by means of *pintles* connected to the *gudgeon* eye fixed on the stern post; steering was by means of a *tiller* handle to the rudder head. Lines or chains (15) secured the rudder to the hull. The rudder appeared in sailing vessels about 1240AD.

• Horizontal windlass and a vertical *capstan* were used to raise, or *sway*, the mast yard and *weigh* the anchor respectively.

• Cargoes carried in the capacious holds of upto 140 tuns, or an average 80 tuns, included the following which contributed to the Hanseatic shipping lines wealth; wine, grain, wool, timber, salted herring, hides, leather, furs, salt, iron and copper ores.

Tunnage

The *tun* was the capacity or volume of a French wine cask of 252 gallon or 1144 litre.

Since the gallon of water weighed 10lbs, a tun of water would weigh 2520lbs.

As the ton weight was equal to 2240lbs, the tun capacity or volume was equated to a ton weight – the difference allowing for wasted space occupied by the irregular shaped tun casks in the hold. All imports were taxed in 1303 according to the ton weight and called *tonnage*.

In 1347 tonnage was replaced by taxation based on the tun, or *tunnage*, reflecting on the trade in wine.

Burthen was the old term for a vessels carrying capacity, expressed as either tunnage or tonnage and remained so until the 18th century.

Decline of the cog and the Hanseatic League came in the late 14th century after almost 200 years of dominating the cargo carrying market – it was displaced by a larger carrier. vessel called the *hulk* which had been developing alongside the cog and mainly used as a carrier in the North Sea. Few if any written records or remains of the hulk exist. In a very short space of time the hulk was to be displaced by yet another type of vessel the product of continuous development in shipbuilding.

Survivors of the cog type vessel, with flat bottom and planked side, were seen during the 1950s in Caernarfonshire beachcraft as the dory kitboat dinghy for use with oars or a small sail. The original *dory* was the hand-lining fishing boat used in the Newfoundland Banks cod fisheries which provided salt cod for Porthmadog schooners.

Derivation of the name cog is open to question; was it derived from the word *cogan* – a basin or bowl, or was it derived from *cwch* a boat, or was cwch derived from *cog*? The *cogge* was an anglo-saxon name for a boat, which was also given to a *cockboat* or small inshore boat.

5. CARAVEL & CARRACK

Caravel

The appearance of Portugese caravels on the Caernarfonshire coast as recorded during the 1460sAD would have been an event of great interest.

The exotic *caravel* would stand out amongst the numerous local small vessels, cogs or hulks, and she would be professionally admired by the local seafarers for the fine weatherly lines of the hull and unusual sail rig and its *three* masts.

Local seafaring at this time was a seasonal affair from around March to October in mainly fair weather on short coast – hugging voyages in vessels, without any particular shelter for the crew who dossed down on the deck, or in bad weather below deck above the cargo, and feeding mainly on salt meat, fish, bread and beer. By contrast the Portugese sailors made all the year voyages of long duration in deepwater, sheltered in stern accommodation and ate cooked food from a galley stove, and sharing in the income their vessel generated. Local seafarers would listen in amazement at the tales of exploration the Portuguese told them of their voyages of discovery along the coast of West Africa.

A few years later in 1485, King Henry VII, worried by the presence of so many foreign vessels shipping wine to Britain, decreed in a Navigation Act that all future wine imports would be only in English, Irish or Welsh vessels. Maybe this provided the stimulus to increase the number of British vessels. Clearly the caravel was the vessel of the future in shipbuilding; consequently the following summarises the main characteristics of the caravel derived mainly from pictures and paintings of the time.

- The caravel originated in 12th century as a small open boat rigged with one mast and a threesided, triangular, *lateen* sail typical of Mediterranean countries. The single masted caravel underwent gradual development into a vessel with fore and aft lateen sails on *two*, then *three* masts, as shown in Figure 9.

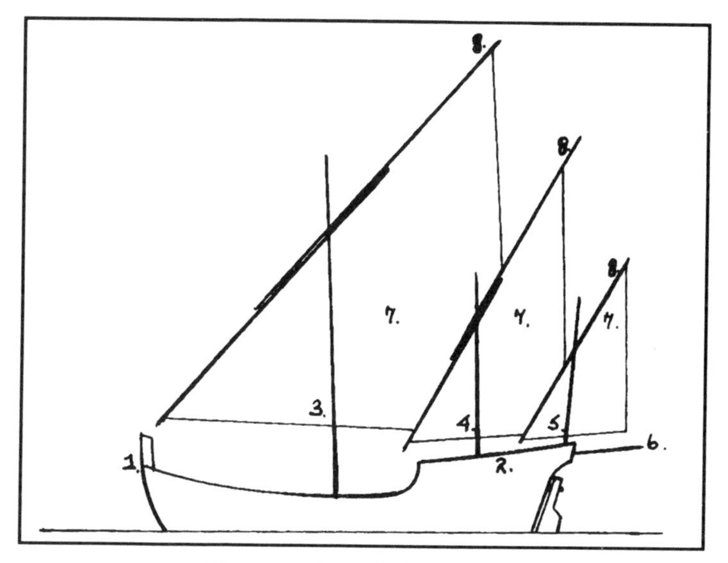

Figure 9. Caravela lateena rig.

• Dimensions; the length varied between 50ft (15m) and 90ft, (28m) with a breadth of 18ft (5.5m), to 24ft (7.4m) and tunnage from 50 to 100tuns.

• The hull was slender and rounded with planks laid edge to edge and fastened into a skeleton framework producing a smooth surfaced strong hull, typical of *carvel* laid planking. (See Figure 17, Plates 7, 9 and 12). The stem post (1) Plate 4 was curved and connected with a keel ending in a vertical or straight stern post. The bows had a hollow or concave *entry or entrance,* offering the least resistance as the vessel stem cut through the sea.

• Early caravels were open without a deck, later caravels had a single upper deck extending the vessels length with openings for cargo hatches. The cargo space was small. Aft there was a *quarter-deck* (2) housing providing shelter and accommodation. *No* castles or structures were located on the mast top, bow, or stern.

• Masts were single pole, see Plate 22, named from the bow as *foremast* (3), *mainmast* (4), and *mizzenmast* (5). An *outrigger* (6) was fitted in the stern and sometimes there would be a bowsprit in the bow, see Plate 21.

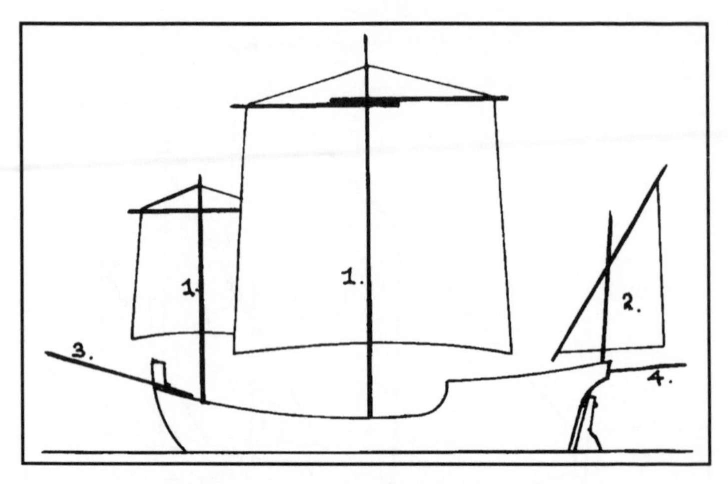

Figure 10. Caravela redonda rig.

- Sails were rigged differently in the two types of caravel:

(a) the *caravela lateena,* had fore and aft lateen sails (7) on each mast connected to a sloping lateen yard (8), as shown in Figure 9.

(b) the *caravela redonda* shown in Figure 10, was a larger three masted caravel with four-sided squaresails (1) on the fore and main masts, and the three-sided lateen sail (2) on the mizzzen mast. Lateen sails helped in steering the vessel, whilst the square sails provided power to drive the vessel. A bowsprit (3) was present together with an outrigger (4). Maybe it was the *caravela redonda* type which visited the Caernarfonshire coast with its cargo of wine.

- Steering was by means of a rudder and tiller. Oars were used in early vessels.
- The caravels sailed with speed, precision and manoeuverability, and together with the shallow draught, or small depth of water needed for the vessel to float in, made them suitable for inshore surveying in shallow coastal waters in voyages of discovery.

Christopher Columbus used both types of caravel in his voyage of discovery of America 1492-1504AD, namely the *caravela lateena, Pinta* and the *caravela redonda, Nina.*

Carrack

The third type of vessel used by Columbus was the forerunner of the *carrack Santa Maria*. This type of vessel first appeared in Britain during the year, 1425AD and displaced the knarr, cog and hulk, becoming the largest and main type of deepsea ship and remained so until the early 1600sAD.

Evidence for the structure of the carrack comes mainly from pictures, and images on pottery and in particular from the remains of the carrack *Mary Rose*, sunk 1545 and raised in 1982.

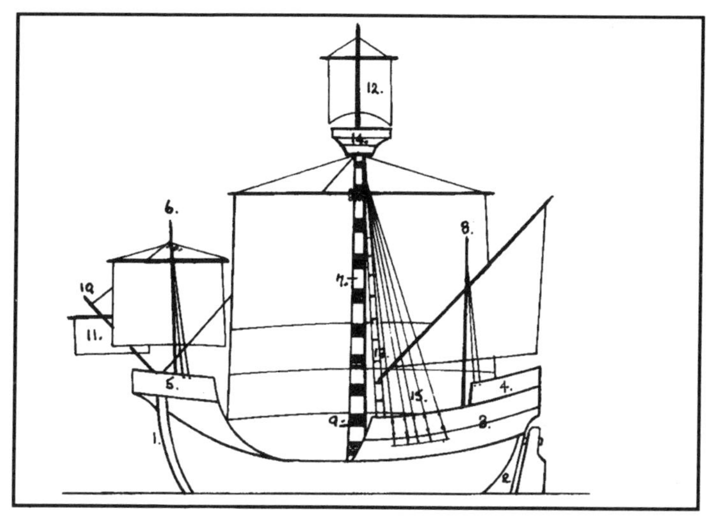

Figure 11. The carrack rig.

The following summarises the main characteristics of the carrack shown in Figure 11. During the the 300 years of its existence it changed in several aspects, particularly size, and in mast and sail rig.

• Dimensions: the carrack varied in length from 67ft (21m) to 115ft (35.5m) and in breadth from 18ft (5.5m) to 34ft (10.5m). The tunnage varied from 100 tuns to over 1000tuns

• Hull was relatively slender, and heavily constructed with thick planks laid edge to edge in *carvel* style fastened to a skeleton framework of frames closely arranged together (see Figure 17). The hull had a deep draught and the hold was capacious for a trading vessel. The stem post (1) was curved and the bows bluff, whilst the stern post (2) was straight and high.

• Sides were high and three wales of thickened planks strengthened the hull lengthwise, *fenders* were also fitted vertically to prevent hull damage alongside stone built quays.

• A single upper deck with hatches in the *well deck* connected with the aftercastle and forecastle at each end. The castles were very high; after castle consisted of a quarter-deck (3) with *half-deck* (4) above, and could also extend to two more decks.; the forecastle (5) projected over the bows.

• Masts varied in number from three to four; from the bow the foremast (6), mainmast (7), mizzenmast (8) and a *bonaventure* mast. The mainmast was very thick, called a *made-mast*, composed of several pieces bound together with rope *wooldings*, or iron bands (9), the other masts were single pole masts. A bowsprit (10) was also present. *Topmasts* were fitted above the lower main mast and foremast in later carracks, each having a saucer-shaped *top* (14).

• Sails:

a) lateen triangular sails were on the mizzen and bonaventure masts.

b) squaresails were on the main, fore and a *bowsprit spritsail* (11) below the bowsprit (The spritsail, since it is attached to the bowsprit should be called the bowsprit sail-with daily usage it was abbreviated to spritsail). *Topsails* (12) were on the main mast topmast, and could also be found on the foremast in later years in larger carracks.

• Rigging became more complex and early carracks had a *jacobs ladder* (13) to the *saucer-shaped top* (14), a small platform at the mainmast head. Later carracks had *ratlines* arranged horizontally on the shrouds (15).

• Steering was by means of *whipstaff* connected to the tiller helm. The steersman operated this staff from the quarterdeck in response to orders shouted to him from the navigating deck.

• The vessel was unweatherly, experiencing side to side rolling in heavy weather, it had poor stability due to the *top hamper* caused by the high hull sides and the tall castles, contributing weight above the waterline. The carrack *Mary Rose* capsized suddenly in 1545, water entering the vessel rapidly through open gun ports.

Replicas

Many former sailing vessel types which have become extinct have now been recreated as replicas. These replica vessels provide information as to their seaworthiness, and sailing abilities .

Plate 37 shows a modern replica of a small *bomb ketch* converted from a carrack type vessel. It is without the foremast, spritsail, and bonaventure mast. It has a staysail and the mizzen is fitted with a topmast and "crosstrees" contrasting with the main masts saucershaped top. The carvel built hull is of the typical carrack form. The vessel shown here is a cargo carrier and is fitted with five gun ports surrounded by decorative wreathes. Decoration is also seen on the stern and stern quarters, this decoration is a forerunner feature of *galleons.* The steering is by means of a tiller.

The main usage of carracks was as exploration vessels, cargo carriers and also as warships fitted with guns on a gun deck or lower deck. Carracks are known to have reached Caernarfonshire carrying wine cargoes.

The decline of the carrack was gradual, the unweatherly, cumbersome, topheavy vessel was replaced by the *galleon.*

Survival

The carvel planked hull has continued to the present day and can be seen in a range of traditionally built wooden boats at Classic Sailboats, Bethel, and at Waterfront Marine, Porth Penrhyn boatyard.

Plate 7 shows the typical carvel hull of a sailing boat undergoing construction at Classic Sailboats, Bethel.

Cymru a'r Môr articles relating to Medieval Welsh shipping include;
"Y llong yn y Canol Oesoedd", K. Lloyd Gruffydd, Vol 13 1990.

"Maritime Wales Export Trade in the later Middle Ages", ditto,Vol 21 ,2000.
"Piracy, Privateering and maritime Wales in the later Middle Ages", ditto, Part one, Vol 24, 2003.
"Piracy, Privateering and maritime Wales during the later Middle Ages" Part two, ditto, Vol 25, 2004.
"Wrecks and wreckers in Welsh waters during the later Middle Ages", ditto, Vol 23, 2002.
"Sea power and the Anglo-Welsh wars 1210-1410", ditto, Vol 11, 1987
"Welsh maritime trade in wine during the Middle Ages", ditto, Vol 15, 1992.
"Maritime defence of Wales during the later Middle Ages", ditto, Vol 18, 1996
"Royal impressment during the later Middle Ages", ditto, Vol 1997-98 .
"Maritime Wales' import trade during the later Middle Ages, Part I", ditto, Vol 27, 2006.
"Maritime Wales' import trade during the later Middle Ages, Part II," ditto, Vol 28, 2007.

6. GALLEONS

Spanish galleons were carrying very rich cargoes from the continent of America – the New World, and this treasure attracted *pirates* to sink the vessels and acquire the cargo. Wealth was being accumulated rapidly, and soon the British government legalised this piracy by issuing licences to individuals or *privateers*. The booty or the profits of this trade, were shared out between the Queen 30%, merchants 30%. the privateer 18% and the other adventurers crew etc received 22%. Prominent amongst these *privateers* was Sir Walter Raleigh, whose piracy expeditions were not very successful, but despite it all he became a favourite of the Queen and something of a national hero.

Amongst Drakes admirers was Pyrs Gruffydd, Esquire of Penrhyn who is said to have built a vessel to sail with Raleigh at the Armada of 1588, whether he did so is open to question. Later it is recorded that in 1600 he was in command of a naval vessel, possibly a small galleon, or fly-boat (fluyt), and engaged as a privateer – a licensed Caernarfonshire pirate!

The *galleon*, Figure 12, was a specific type of vessel which developed from and ultimately displaced the carrack. The larger Spanish galleon was the basic template which led to the development, during 1570s, of the smaller *English galleon*, a vessel which became the main trading and warship for the next two hundred years. The name galleon was never used in Britain for this essentially English vessel, instead it was known as a *man-of-war* or *merchantman*.

Evidence for the structure of galleons abounds in the paintings of English and Dutch artists and from models, and in the remains of the galleon *Wasa*, sunk in 1627 and raised in 1961 to be displayed in Stockholm.

The 16th century was the age of scientists, Galileo and Newton, who contributed to the science of navigation; whilst knowledge of ship structure was being recorded in the ship drawings of Mathew Baker a naval draughtsman. Here then in the 16th century was the starting point of *our* maritime heritage.

The main structural characteristics of the English galleon, Figure 12, are summarised as follows:

• Dimensions ranged from 135ft (42m) to 210ft (65m) length; and 33ft (10m) to 43ft (13m) breadth; these dimensions indicate the hull was comparitively narrow, and much more slender than the carrack. Ship constructors found that long narrow hulls produced speedy vessels.

• Tunnage varied from around 50 to 200 and upto 1200 tuns.

• Hull construction of all galleons from 1550AD, and all future large sailing vessels, was in the style of carvel planking laid edge to edge, and fastened to an underlying pre-erected skeleton framework of keel, stem and stern posts connecting with the timbers, see Plates 1, 3, 4, 7, 8 and 9, also Figure 17 and 25. This method of construction produced a strong hull, and vessel size was almost unlimited, in comparison to the clincher built hull which became restricted to small sailing vessels.

• The bow was round and bluff, resembling a cods head, and the stern flattened from side to side like a mackerels tail, this fishlike hull form would allow the hull to move easily through the water. See Plates 12 and 13. Hull sides had a *tumble-home*, or sides which sloped inwards towards the ship centre line.

• Upperworks above the waterline are considerably reduced in comparison to the carrack, this reduction produces a more stable vessel, and less top hamper. Figure 12 shows, the stern is a flat transom, composed a quarter-deck (1) and half-deck (2), providing accommodation for officers. Whilst the forecastle is greatly reduced to become an integral part of the hull and within the bows instead of being outside as in a carrack. A prominent feature is the *beakhead* (3) connected to the stem head and functions as the crews w. c. or "heads" – in addition it allowed access to the bowsprit headsails. At the stern is a *gallery* (4) or balcony – an extension of officers accommodation and their toilets. In later vessels the hull was decorated extensively with carvings, sculptures and much gilt in addition to the prominent figurehead – the whole thing resembling a travelling fairground side show! Later vessels in the

1660sAD reduced all this ostentation.

• Decks in warships, the men-of war, commenced above the hold as the *orlop deck*, or, the lowest deck, above which was the gun or *lower deck*, then the upper deck with its quarter-deck and half-deck and focsle deck. Guns had formerly contributed to vessel instability and their number was reduced from about 250 in carracks to less than 100 in English galleons, or men-of -war.

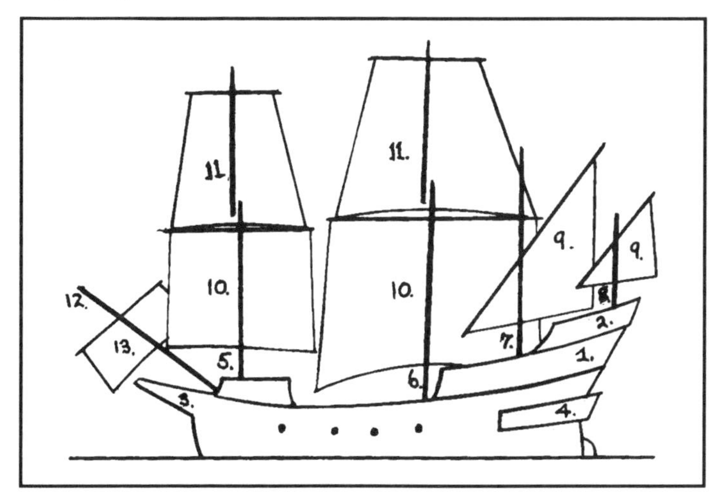

Figure 12. Early English galleon rig.

• Masts totalled four, as shown in Figure 12, and were made-masts bound with rope wooldings or iron bands. From the bow they were named as: foremast (5), mainmast (6), single pole mast of the mizzenmast (7) and the bonaventure mast (8).

The early English galleons during the 16th century had *two part* masts composed of *lower mast*, and *top mast* as shown in Figure 12. Later vessels had a third part – the *topgallant mast*. All mast parts overlapped and were bound together at the *doublings* (see Figure 28). In the Conwy records for 1577 there are three vessels of under a hundred tuns collectively called "topmen" – it could be assumed that these were galleon type vessels with masting composed of the lower mast and *topmast* – hence the name "topmen".

• Sails were cut flat from canvas and were not of the billowing type used in carracks.

a) lateen sails (9), spread on lateen yards, were set on the mizzen and bonaventure mast;
b) main and fore masts had squaresails (10) and *topsails* (11). Later topgallant sails and studding sails were added. Royal sails appeared in 1637 above the topgallant sails. (Details of these and other sails are dealt with in later chapters, 13, 14, and 15.)
c) the bowsprit (12) had a square spritsail (13) – or bowsprit sail.
e) *staysails* appeared in 1660sAD.

• Steering was by means of a tiller and whipstaff, then the *steering wheel* took over in 1705.

• Rigging both standing and running developed as the masting and sails increased. *Ratlines,* see Figure 29, and Plates 24, 28, 29 and 32 were now common on the shrouds, these allowed crews to climb upto the the yards and handle the sails.

The English galleon was the *prototype* for developing the vessels of the future, from it and during the next 200 years

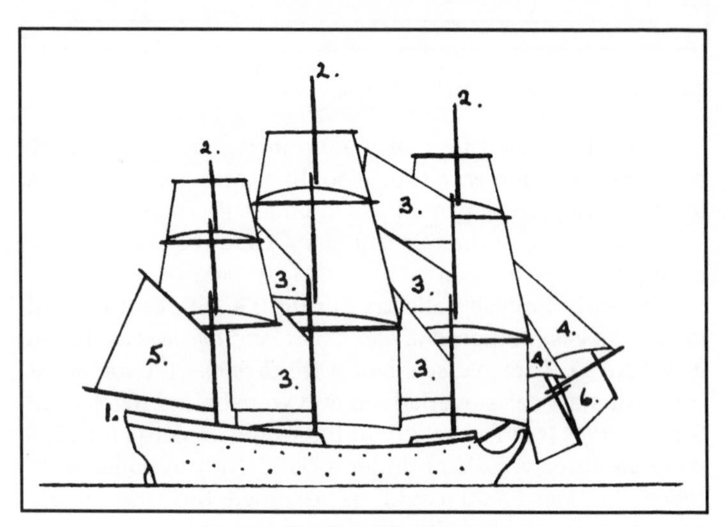

Figure 13. A merchantman rig.

vessels were produced which were seaworthy, stable, fast and manouverable to become the Men-of-War and the merchantmen of the latter 18th century, and clipper ships of the 19th century.

Merchantman

Merchantman: Figure 13. This vessel retained the basic English galleon hull structure with the quarter deck (1) being enlarged.

• The masting consisted of three part masts, and the number of sails were increased with topgallant masts (2) and topgallant sails.

• *Mast staysails* (3) appeared between the masts, and *headsails* (4) were located between the foremast and bowsprit. The mizzen lateen was replaced by a *gaff sail* (5), see Figure 39, and bonaventure mast was removed entirely. For a short time a *spritsail topsail* (6) existed above the bowsprit *spritsail*.

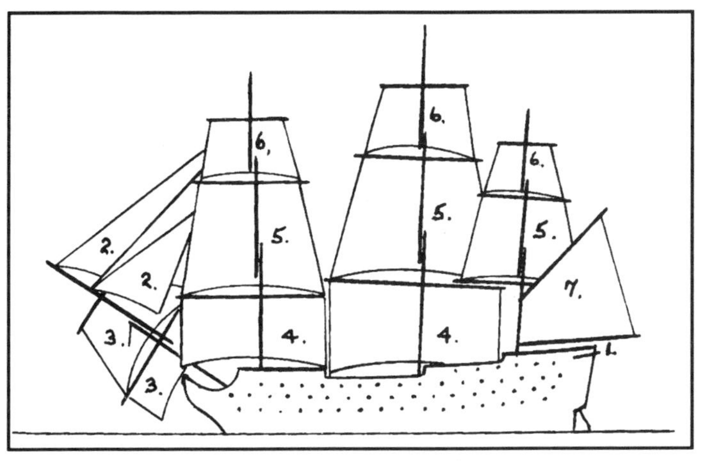

Figure 14. A man-of-war. Ship of the line rig.

Man-of-war

• The man-of-war Figure 14 was the naval vessel, also called a ship of the line in later years. It retained the basic English galleon hull structure together with several decks to accommodate the armaments. In addition the *half-deck* (1) was enlarged.

- The masting was similar to the merchantman with fore, main and mizzen masts all masts composed of *three* parts; lower mast, topmast and topgallant mast.
- The sail rig consisted of:

a) *headsails* (2), two: a jib and outer jib; together with spritsails (3), the upper one called a spritsail topsail. The spritsail topsail was rigged to a spritsail topmast, this became extinct after 1720 and replaced by the jib-boom. (Note: *headsails* are all those sails set or hoisted at the forward end of a vessel-jibs, staysails and spritsails.)

b) *squaresails*: included; lower mast squaresails or *courses* (4), square topsails (5), and topgallant sails (6).

c) *gaff sails*: a single gaff sail (7).

English Galleons of Note

Mayflower, this was a small 180 tun, galleon type of vessel that took the Pilgrim Fathers to New England, in 1620.

Golden Hind, the small galleon in which Sir Francis Drake circumnavigated the Earth from 1577 to 1580.

HMS Clio, stationed in the Menai Strait 1877-1920, a former man-of-war, or ship of the line, known as a 3rd rater or frigate-she was an industrial training school for young boys, also known locally as the workhouse.

HMS Conway, stationed on the Menai Strait, during 1940s, a former man-of-war type galleon, ship of the line, known as a 2nd rater – she was a cadet training school for the MN and RN.

HMS Victory, built 1759 as a 1st rater, ship of the line, participated in the Battle of Trafalgar, and was crewed by many Welshmen under Lord Nelson.

Cymru a'r Môr articles relating to English galleons etc include:
"The *Conway*" and North Wales, Capt. Gwyn. D. Pari Huws, Volume 1, 1976.
"Establishing the *Clio*", E.W. Roberts, Vol 7, 1984.
"Twentyfour Welshmen at Trafalgar", David Ellison, Vol 14, 1991.

7. SLOOPS

The single masted, cargo carrying, sailing vessel called a *trading sloop* appeared in the 1600s. An armed naval version engaged in customs and anti-smuggling duties was called a *revenue cruiser* or *revenue sloop*. Pictorial evidence and plans of these vessels are scarce. The Frontispiece* shows two sloops opposite Caernarfon castle. Records for sloops appear in Appendix 2 of David Thomas, *Hen Longau Sir Gaernarfon* and date from the 1750s.

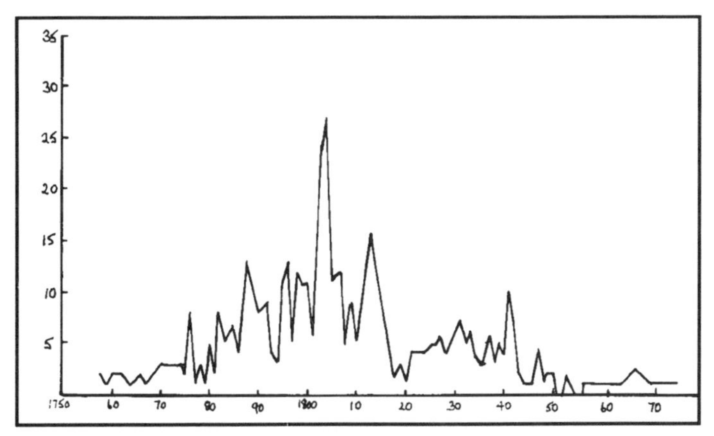

Figure 15.
Number of sloops built in Caernarfonshire 1750-1910.

The graph, Figure 15, shows that over 570 sloops were built in Caernarfonshire – almost half this number were built in Pwllheli – during the period 1750 to 1910. Pwllheli maintained the reputation as a builder of sloops by selling over 60% of its total production outside the county.

The sloop was the most common type of wooden sailing vessel built in the county, rivalled only by the schooner in later years.

The period 1795 to 1820 was a period of war with France during which many Caernarfonshire sloops and other vessels were taken by French privateers, an activity which came to a halt following the defeat of the French at Trafalgar in 1805. The following are some of the Caernarfonshire sloops taken by French privateers: *Catherine* 92t 1784 Llanbedrog; *Bridget* 50t 1796, Caernarfon; *Felicity* 41t 1796 Pwllheli; *Syren* 73 t 1786 Dwyfor Abercin.

The peak of sloop building was reached in 1803 this was followed by a period of gradual decline and replacement by new types of sailing vessels, which were faster and had a larger cargo capacity than the sloops and were more able to cater for the expanding trade of the time.

The new harbour at Porthmadog was opened in 1824 and the building of sloops ceased from 1850s. Trade and the economy in general continued to expand and improve from the 1820s. Meanwhile the marine steam engine was developed in 1820.

The typical characteristics of the sloop are summarised as follows:

• The average dimensions; 36.5ft (11m) length x 13ft (4m) breadth x 6.5ft (2m) depth.

• The *numerical ratios* derived from a vessels dimensions are calculated as follows; *length/breadth* (L/B) ratio 36. 5/13 = 2.8; *breadth/depth* (B/D) 13/6. 5 = 2.

These ratios give indications as to the hull *form*. When the L/B ratio is **2.6** or less it indicates a *beamy* hull; a ratio of more than **3.75** indicates a *narrow* hull. Similarly when the B/D ratio is less than **2.0** it indicates a *deep* hull; a ratio of over **3.0** indicates a *shallow* hull.

The calculated ratios indicate that the *sloop* hull is relatively beamy and deep.

• Tonnage net, was registered for all vessels over 15 ton – this was in accordance with the Act of 1786. The graph, Figure 16, showing tonnage of all sloops built in Caernarfonshire during 1750 to 1910 and indicates an average value for a sloop tonnage as being 28.5 ton net.

• In general the trading sloop appears as a *short, beamy* and *deep* vessel as confirmed from examination of pictorial evidence. See Plates 38, 39 and 40 and frontispiece.

• The hull had a bluff bow, or cods head and mackerel tail, connected to a square transom stern. The revenue sloop had a sharper bow and finer lines compared to the trading

VESSEL CONSTRUCTION

Plate 1. **Centreline Structure**; A new sailing boat begins construction at Classic Sailboats, Bethel. The centreline structure, consists L to R; the transom, sternpost, after deadwood, keel, and stem. The keel is supported by triangular stocks on ground, and shores connected to roof, together with temporary gramps between transom and sternpost and deadwood and keel. (AUTHOR)

Plate 2. **Keel preparation**; the new forward section of the keel of a nobby undergoing restoration at Porth Penrhyn boatyard. The picture shows the curve towards the stem and the straight portion to connect with the existing keel. Notches are being cut out to take the floor timbers. (Mike Arridge, Pentir)

Plate 3. **Transom preparation**; of a new sailing boat at Classic Sailboats, Bethel, shows the raked transom is composed of two parts with a hardwood tongue in the joint, the sternpost is cramped in position together with the after deadwood below. (AUTHOR)

Plate 4. ***Stem preparation****; the stem is of laminated construction from the stem head to the keel scarph, the inner portion is the stem apron. Shores provide support from stem to the building roof at Classic Sailboats, Bethel.*
(AUTHOR)

Plate 5. ***Bow section****; of a fully planked hull being restored at Classic Sailboats, Bethel. The new partly replaced upper sheerstrake and the partly replaced garboard strake are visible.*
(AUTHOR)

Plate 6. ***Stern section****; of a fully planked hull being restored at Classic Sailboats, Bethel. The planks connect with the transom as plank ends. The lowest garboard strake is next to a space where the plank has been removed, and a damaged plank is next to the bilge strake.*
(AUTHOR)

*Plate 7. **New hull**; the planked up hull of a new sailing boat at Classic Sailboats, Bethel. The darker top plank or sheerstrake contrasts with the lighter coloured wood of the carvel laid planking. The deck beams are being inserted. Note the sheer clamp running from the inner side of the bow to stern.*
(AUTHOR)

*Plate 8. **Frames**; Scott Metcalfe, proprietor of Waterfront Marine, amongst the ribs, these are composed of frame and lower floor timbers, sawn from selected curved grain stock of oak wood, the floors are braced across the keel and bolted through the keel with galvanised iron bolts. The hull is being renovated and all perished frames have been removed, whilst the old carvel planking later to be removed and replaced, is visible behind the new frames.*
(Mike Arridge, Pentir)

Plate 9. ***Deck beams****; have been completely fitted. Note the darker coloured sheer-strake and the inner sheer clamp, with frame heads and spacing blocks in between. The stem is of oak, the hull planking is of larch fastened with zinc galvanised iron boat nails or spikes. This is a small cutter or nobby, undergoing complete renovation at the Waterfront Marine boatyard, Porth Penrhyn.*
(Mike Arridge, Pentir.)

Plate 10. ***Decking;*** *of douglas fir being sprung into place, each deck plank connects by way of a tongue and groove seen in plank endview. The plank upper open seam is later payed, or filled. with the modern equivalent of white lead putty- polyurethane sealing compound. Each deck plank is bedded down into sealing compound and screwed to the deck beams.*
(Mike Arridge, Pentir)

Plate 11. ***Decking complete;*** *the cockpit space has a a coaming of larch together with an iroko wood capping. The mast hole is visible abaft of the large oak, samson post. The outer coaming or deck rail is being fitted starting at the aft section, or taffrail, using dark coloured iroko wood. The upper sheer-strake has a scribing line carved on it lenghtwise, later the boats name will be carved also, below this strake is the moulding, or rubbing strake.*
(Mike Arridge, Pentir)

Plate 12. ***Bow and stem****; the stem is a typical cutter stem with its cutwater which divides or cuts the water before it reaches the bow. The sharp bow has a slight hollowing, also known as the fine entrance, or entry, being the underwater form of the bow, allowing the vessel to thrust its way through the sea. Caulking is taking place on the stem seams, the twisted cotton caulking is treated with polyurethane sealing compound, previously white lead putty was used. The outer coaming or rail has been fitted completely and the scupper hole is visible. (Mike Arridge, Pentir.)*

Plate 13. ***Stern structure;*** *the stern is rounded and called an ellipitical counter stern, the counter being the overhang betwen the stern and waterline. The stern-post is below the counter stern. The run aft is clearly seen as the graceful under-water stern form; this clean run allows the hull to slip through the water with the least resistance. The stern nogs, or timber bitts, are visible on the after deck, they are hitching posts for trawl lines. The boat is resting on its bilge where the bilge strake is thicker than the other hull strakes. (Mike Arridge. Pentir)*

Plate 14. ***Schooner on stocks****; the skeletal framework of a schooner under construction at Porthmadog circa 1900. Note the massive frames and their close positioning. The framework is supported by shores, whilst the keel rest on blocks or stocks. The square stern is being shaped by means of fashion pieces to form a transom stern counter. (Gwynedd Archives)*

Plate 15. ***Planked hull****; the schooner hull is approaching complete planking. The surface of the carvel planking is bristling with treenails waiting to be cut away fair with the surface. The frame heads project upwards and may be used as bulwark stanchions. (Gwynedd Archives)*

Plate 16. ***Steel hull contstruction;*** *the steel hull of a barquentine "Leeuwin", under construction at Fremantle, West Australia. Not its stern post, and counter stern, together with steel shores and the block framework to support the vessels keel. The vessel hull has a pronounced deadrise.*
(Author)

Plate 17. ***Samson post;*** *this post passes through the deck and is secured to the keel, it provides a means to secure the mooring lines, and backs up the heel of the bowsprit.*
(Author)

Plate 18. ***Focsle companion****; this is the covering hatchway to the focsle accommodation and connects with a ladder or companionway.*
(Author)

Plate 19. ***After companion****; this is the hatchway covering leading into the main after cabin accoomodation, and also functions as a skylight. A companionway or staircase ladder leads downwards.*
(Author)

Plate 20. ***Steering wheel;*** *connects with the steering housing; in the background the stanchions are seen supporting the bulwarks and capping rail. Mooring lines are made fast to the cavils.*
(Author)

Plate 21. ***Bowsprit;*** *the bowsprit is made from locally grown douglas fir. The taper of this spar is being checked with a rule. The heel of the bowsprit abuts against the samson post or goes between the bitts, depending on the type of vessel, in this case small cutter or nobby built at Waterfront Marine, Porth Penrhyn.*
(Mike Arridge, Pentir)

Plate 22. ***Mast;*** *a single pole mast of douglas fir upto 40 ft is being tapered with a plane and spokeshave. It will be later stepped in the nobby at the Porth Penrhyn boatyard. The hull in the background has been completely caulked and sealed.* *(Mike Arridge, Pentir)*

Plate 23. ***Deadeyes****; wooden blocks with three holes which have lanyards roved through them. They serve to tauten the shrouds and backstays. Also seen is a small pin rail with lines belayed. (Author)*

Plate 24. ***Rigging screws****; these are also called turnscrews and bottlescrews, used to tauten the shrouds and backstays. (Author)*

Plate 25. ***Yards****; two yards are seen fixed to the single pole fore mast of a small topsail schooner by means of trusses and steel swivels. The single pole mast is 45 ft high and has a maximun diameter of 11 inches. (Author)*

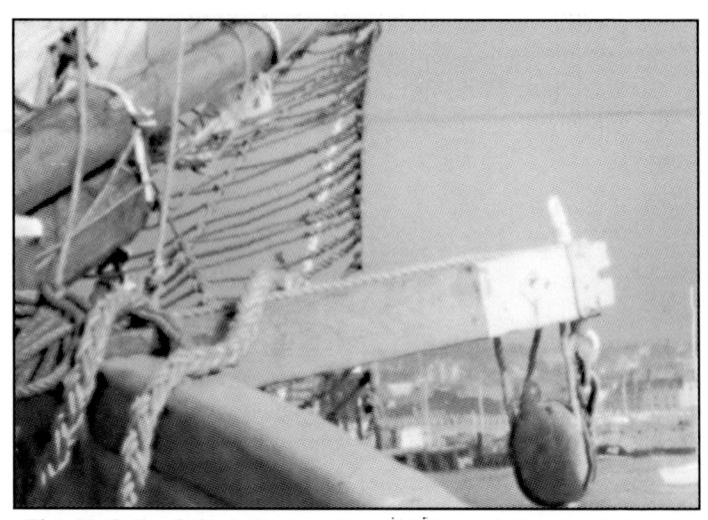

Plate 26. ***Cathead****; this is the strong beam of timber projecting over the bow. Its purpose is to hold the stock of an anchor before letting go, or to hold it, before securing the anchor on its bed after weighing. (Author)*

Plate 27. ***Gaff****; the gaff sail luff connects with the mast by means of wooden sail hoops made from strips of oakwood steamed into shape and copper rivetted. The gaff spar throat connects with the mast by means of the gaff jaws and the parrel beads. The gaff boom connects with the mast by way of the steel gooseneck universal joint and its mast bands. (Author)*

Plate 28. ***Brig tops****; of the brig "Royalist"are seen from abaft, or the mast after-side view. The two tops of the main mast are approached by means of the lower and upper ratline shrouds. The upper top has ratline shrouds to the mast head. The gaff spar connects with the mast by way of a shoe and track. (Author)*

Plate 29. ***Brig Sails****; seen from abaft, or the foremast afterside view. The sails are named as the fore course sail, the upper topsail, and the topgallant sail. The mast is a single pole structure. The gaff boom is seen in the lower foreground right. (Author)*

Plate 30. ***Brig sails;*** *the main mast sails of the brig "Royalist" seen from afore the mast, show the set topsail and set topgallant sails.*
In the foreground is the main topmast staysail with its luff connected to the stay by hanks.
(Author)

Plate 31. ***Masthead assembly;*** *The foremast of the brigantine is composed of three parts. The lower masthead assembly is seen together with its top composed of a rim with decking supported by crosstrees. The stronger fore and aft trestletrees are seen above the mast head cheeks. The topmast heel is rectangular and can be seen between the mast head cheeks. The cap is just visible holding the the head of the lower mast to the lower part of the topmast.(Author)*

Plate 32. ***Brigantine sails;*** *Centre is the foremast of the brigantine "Soren Larsen", this is a three part mast and has a top and "crosstrees". The sails to be seen in this afterside view are ; the topgallant sail, the upper topsail, and part of the lower topsail. The left of the picture shows the luff of the gaff sail connected to the main mast by means of wooden hoops, the gaff spar jaws are to be seen connecting with the mast, below the "crosstrees". (Author)*

Plate 33. ***Brigantine foremast****; The foremast sails from below upwards are; the fore course sail, the lower topsail, the upper topsail, and the topgallant sail. The top right corner shows the fore topmast staysail. The buntlines are seen to extend from the squaresail head to the foot. (Author)*

VESSEL TYPES

Plate 34. ***Scandinavian clincher vessels, c 1066****; The Bayeux Tapestry consisting of embroidered linen, measuring 231ft (69m) in length, illustrates the invasion of England by the Normans. This portion shows the vessels used were of the Scandinavian type ; one unloading horses had a hoistable sail. The other beached vessels were evidently propelled entirely by oars.*
(Ville De Bayeux)

Plate. 35. ***Shetland fouren****; this model of a Shetland fouren is from the Nautical Museum, Castletown, Isle Of Man. It shows the Scandinavian influence, as the Shetland Isles were under Scandinavian rule for over 600 years. This type of vessel continues to be used in Shetland as an inshore fishing boat.*
The hull is clinker built and is propelled by a lugsail, and four oars and steered by a long tiller. (Author)

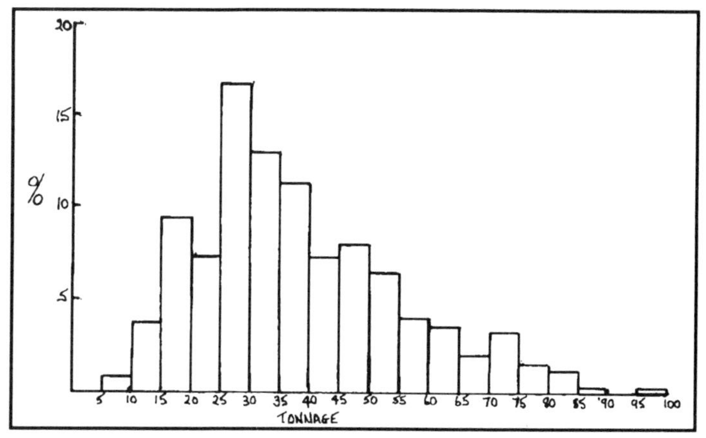

Figure 16. Sloop tonnage ,Caernarfonshire 1750-1910.

sloop; its distinguishing feature was the vessels ornately carved and high stern.

• Hull construction: the larger wooden sailing vessels built from the 1650s followed the method of skeleton sequence of construction in which a framework of keel, stempost, sternpost and timbers was first erected to produce the hull shape, see Figure 25 and Plates 1, 3, 4 and 8. The keel was laid on top of *blocks* and the sides and bottom of the timbers, or *frames*, were supported by *shores*, meanwhile the stern frame was built on to the stern post; when all the frames or timbers were in place the vessel was at the in-frame stage, or on the *stocks* as shown in Plate 14.

Later the skeleton framework was *planked up* by laying the planks in an edge to edge fashion, carvel style, fastened through into the skeleton framework by means of metal nails or wooden treenails. See Plates 7 and 9. When all the planks or strakes had been laid and fastened, the outer surface would appear bristling with treenail heads, as shown in Plate 15.

• Figure 17 shows sectional view of carvel built hulls. The skeleton timbers, frames, also called ribs (1), are shown each side and connected to the keel (2) and *keelson* (3). Parts of the timbers connected to the keel are called *floors* (4), and the other pieces called the *futtock timbers* (5) and *top timbers*

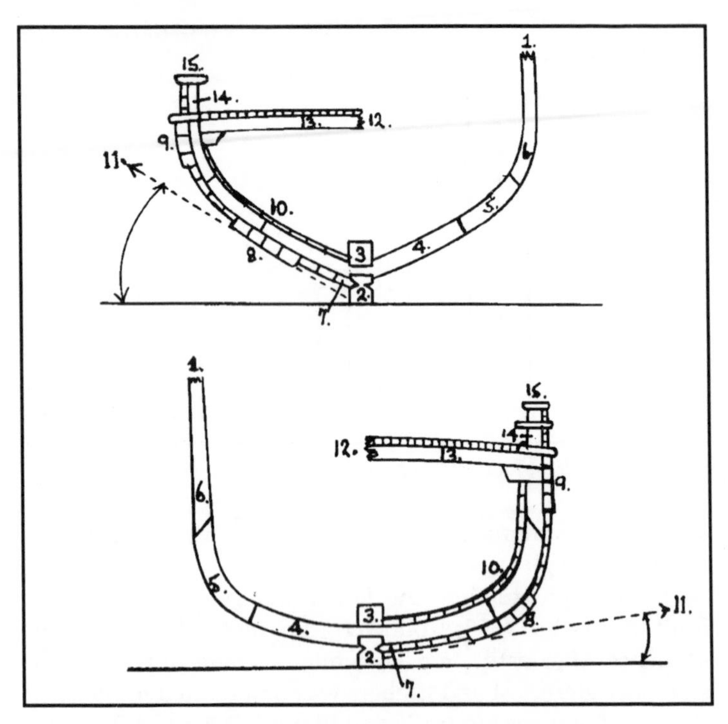

Figure 17. Carvel hull midsection structure.

(6). See Plate 8. A complete *frame* would be composed of the different timbers parts on the port and starboard sides of the keel.

• Planking next to the keel is the garboard strake (7), whilst certain strakes are thicker in the lower *wales* (8) near the bilge, or bulge; and the upper side wales or rubbing strakes (9). See Plates 5 and 6. Ceiling planking (10) lines the hold to prevent damage from heavy cargoes such as stones.

• The advantages of a skeleton constructed hull are: it can be used for larger and stronger hulled vessels; quicker and cheaper method of construction; easier to maintain and repair; ideal for heavily armed vessels or heavy cargo carriage.

• The *deadrise* (11) of a hull is shown by means of an arrow in the Figure 17. The upper hull has a steep deadrise, in a *rounded* hull, which will cause the vessel to heel over on its side when taking the ground. See Plates 13 and 48. The lower hull has smaller deadrise, or a *flat* bottom, this allows the vessel to remain upright on taking the ground. Sloops had relatively flat bottoms and were able to take the ground easily in most coastal places. See Plates 39 and 40.

• The upper deck (12) extends the vessels full length with openings for the cargo hatches, decking planks are laid on the deck beams (13). See Plates 7, 9, 10 and 11. Low *bulwarks* composed of planking fastened to *stanchions*, or top timbers (14) have a main *capping rail* (15). See Plate 20.

• Masting of the sloop consisted of a single pole mast in the early vessels, Plate 22, and was composed of a *two part* mast in later sloops of the 1820s; the topmast could be lowered or reeved, see Plate 40. The mast was stepped a third of the length from the bows. The bowsprit was sloping, or had a *steeving*; it was also fixed, or standing, meaning it could not be drawn, or reeved, into the vessel. Sloops had a *taffrail* or stern rail aft (1) as shown in the following Figure 18, and in the Frontispiece.

The sail rig of a revenue sloop and a trading sloop are shown in Figure 18.

• The trading sloop rig Figure 18 (a), see also Plate 40, consisted of:

a) *headsails* (2): usually one hanked to the forestay, fixed to the bowsprit end, and a second headsail for use in fair weather.

b) *gaff sails*: a single *gaff sail* (3), together with a *gaff topsail* (4). Some trading sloops had a single square topsail on a hoisting yard for use in fair weather.

• The revenue and naval sloop Figure 18 (b), had a greater sail area handled by a bigger crew and was similar to the trading sloop but included an extra headsail (2), together with a square mainsail (6), also called a *running squaresail*, connected to a fixed spreader yard; this was a fair weather sail used when running before the wind.

The square topsail (3) was connected to a fixed topsail yard; whilst the upper topsail (5) was connected to a hoisting yard; all of which contributed to its greater sail area and speed compared to the trading sloop.

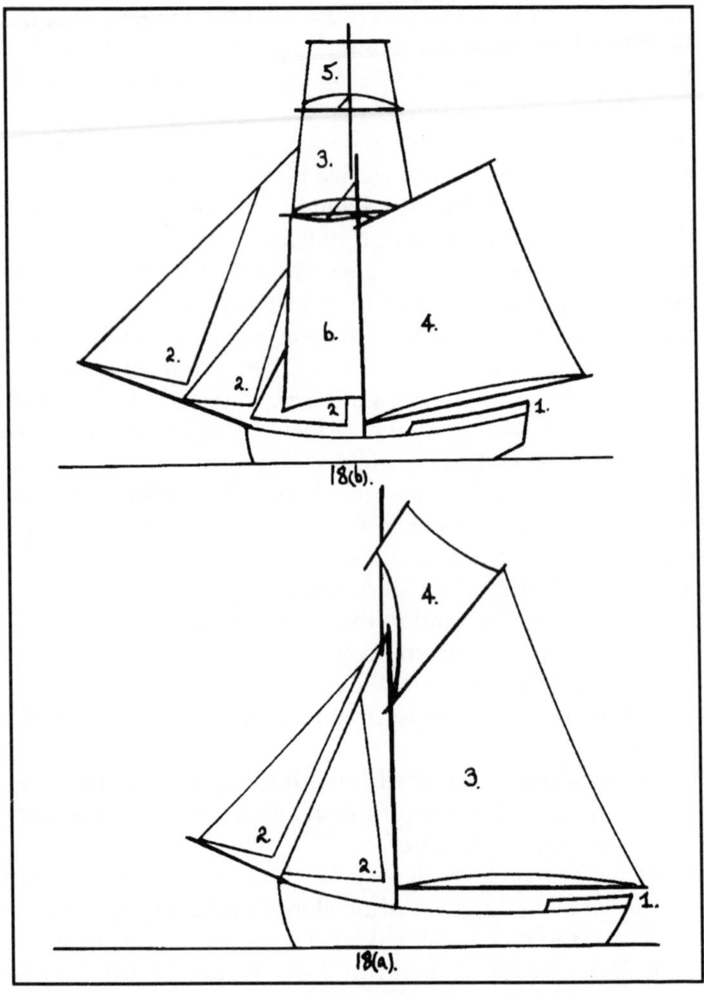

Figure 18.
Revenue sloop rig (above), trading sloop rig (below).

• Trading sloops were found in almost every port and creek in Caernarfonshire see Plates 38, 39 and 40, and their trading voyages were short and mainly within Wales or to England, with the remainder to Ireland, Scotland and Isle of Man.

Acts aimed at prevention of smuggling covered all types

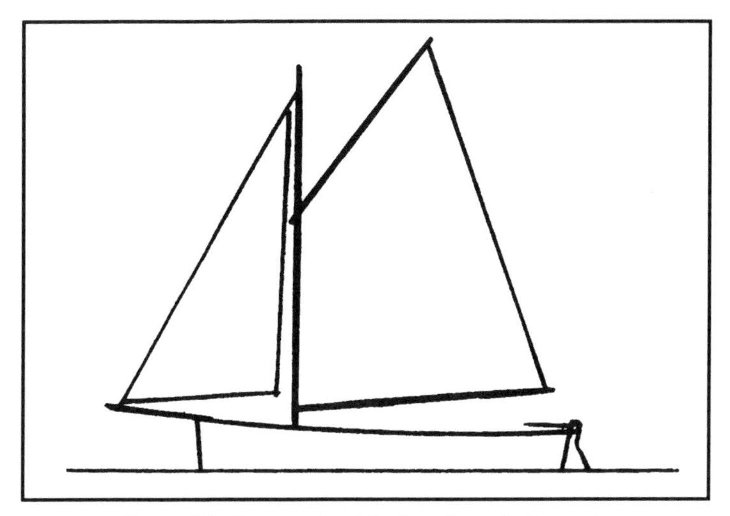

Figure 19. Caernarfonshire beach craft-sloop rig.

of vessels except trading sloops which were regarded as too slow for this activity.

• A trading sloop of note for its longevity was the *Jenny,* 27ft (8.3m) length x 11.9ft (3.6m) breadth x 6.3 (1.9m) depth, 20t, built Nefyn 1787, wrecked 1919 at the great age of 132 years!

• The *average life* of a wooden sailing vessel, terminated by fire, wood decay or wreck, was between 30 and 37 years.

• Sloops were suitable vessels for conversion into steamer craft by installation of a steam engine. The sloop *Temple,* built at Trefriw 1874 was converted into a steam vessel in 1932 – after 58 years in sail!

• Revenue and naval sloops were featured in old paintings of Caernarfon – they had a distinct high ornate stern-resembling a miniature English galleon together with an ensign on an ensign staff.

• Sloops were often converted into schooners e.g. the *Petrel* of Bangor and *General Havelock* of Conwy.

• Beach craft in Caernarfonshire upto the 1950s, in Aberdaron, Nefyn and other harbours and creeks in Llŷn were of simple sloop type rig, as in Figure 19. They had a wooden clincher built hull with a sharp straight bow and square transom stern. There was a small cuddy with deck forward and other boats were completely decked but for an open cockpit.

Survival

Gaff rigged sloops are still being built in Gwynedd at Classic Sailboats, Bethel. These lovely little vessels keep sailing alive in various parts of Wales today.

Cymru a'r Môr articles relating to the sloop include:
"Survey and excavation of sloop *Lovely*", Butland W. E., and Stubbs J. M.,Vol 1, 1976.
"The Welsh Sloop", M. K. Stammers, Vol 21, 2000.
"The flight of the *Raven*", ditto, Vol 22, 2001.
"The *Ann and Susan* of Porthmadog", Penri Davies, Vol 4, 1979.
"The sloop *Darling*, Beaumaris 1781-1893," O. T. P. Roberts, Vol 7, 1983.
"The sloop *Jenny*, 1787-1919", M. Ellis-Williams, Vol 10, 1986.

8. SMACKS

According to data in Appendix 2 of D. Thomas, *Hen Longau Sir Gaernarfon* over eighty vessels, described as *smacks,* were built in the county during the period 1832 to 1872. The peak period of building was reached in 1848 following an upsurge in trade and improved economy after the French wars; this is shown in the graph, Figure 20. Comparing this graph with Figure 15 for the total sloops built in Caernarfonshire, the decline of sloop building coincided with the *rise* in smack building. Evidently the popularity of sloops was favoured by the *Navigation Acts* of 1773 and 1784, aimed at preventing smuggling, which encouraged slow sailing vessels and restricted the sailing ability of other vessels in the hope they would be caught by the faster revenue cruisers. Relaxation of this law in the 1820s, encouraged the building of fast sailing vessels which were needed generally for overseas trading and to support the booming economy. Meanwhile

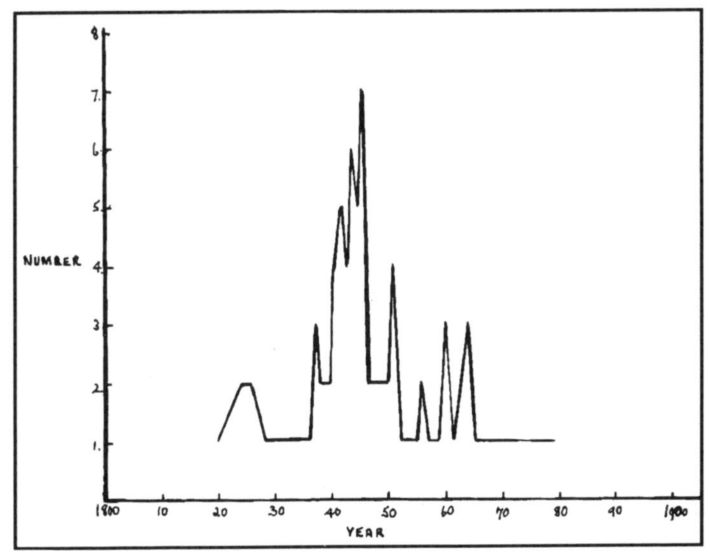

Figure 20.
Number of smacks built in Caernarfonshire 1800-1900.

smuggling and impressment by the press gangs continued until the late 1850s.

Navigation Acts embraced various seafaring activities ranging from, eating fish on Wednesday and Saturday; coaster crews to be made up of 75% English speaking master and crew, in later years altered to 25% English speaking master and crew; followed by the compulsory examination of masters and mates in 1850, and the whack system of feeding crews in 1854. The act of 1651 prohibited the import of goods on foreign ships.

Evidence for the structure of smacks comes mainly from pictorial records, but these are scanty as the vessels were small and maybe did not merit particular attention. Owners had models and paintings many of which were over embellished.

J. Glyn Davies (1870-1953) author of *Cerddi Porth Dinllaen* delighted in the sights of smacks in his boyhood circa 1880-85, see Plate 49. To complicate the issue the name was subject to change; the Liverpudlians called the Welsh smacks – cutters!

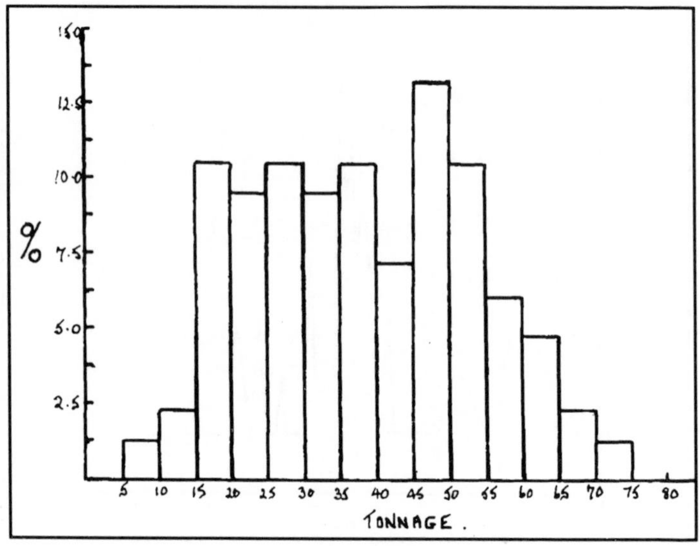

Figure 21.
Smack tonnage, Caernarfonshire 1800-1900.

The characteristic features of Caernarfonshire smacks (Plate 41) are summarised as follows;

• The average dimension of a smack is: 39.7ft (12.1m) length x 13.26ft (4m) breadth x 6.17ft (1.9m) depth.

• The calculated length/breadth ratio = 2.99, and the breadth/depth ratio = 2.14. This indicates a fairly beamy and deep vessel. In comparison to a sloop the smack shows a slight reduction in breadth, and slightly less depth ratio.

• The smack tonnage values are shown in the graph, Figure 21, within a range from 5 to 75 ton and having an average value of 38 ton, an increase of 33% compared to the average sloop tonnage value of 28.5 ton. The smack shown in Figure 22, evidently was a larger vessel than the sloop.

• The carvel planked hull has a straight stem (1), and the bows are bluff; the stern (2) is a flat transom with a *counter* beneath. Plates 3 and 6. The hull is full bodied and deep to the keel; a moderate deadrise allowed the vessel to heel over when discharging cargo on a beach. See Plate 48. A low bulwark is present. By the 1840s the carvel style of planking in all wooden large sailing vessels had displaced the clincher style entirely, apart from its use in small rowing and sailing

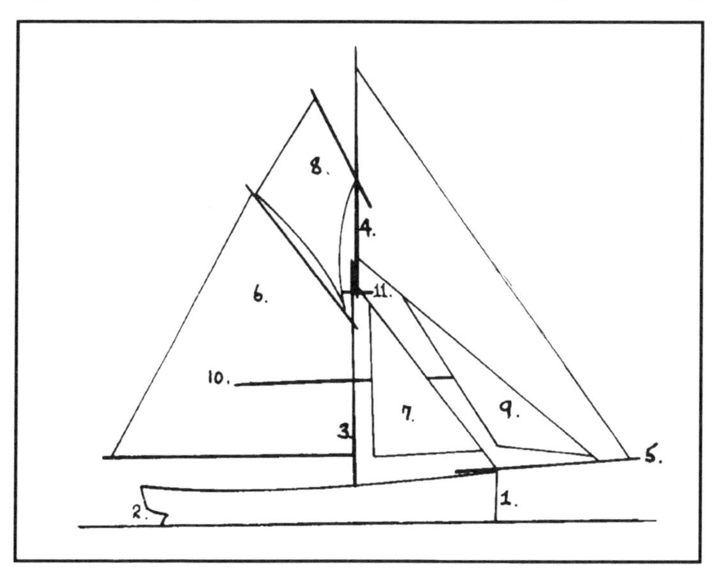

Figure 22. Trading smack rig.

vessels.

• An upper deck extends the vessel length with a hatchway to a gear and sail store below deck forward in the focsle, and crew accommodation in larger smacks aft in a small cabin. The cargo hatchway opens into a large ceiling lined hold.

• A single, two part mast, consisting of lower mast (3) and topmast (4), together with *"crosstrees"* at the doublings, see Figure 28; was stepped one third the deck length from the stem.

• The running bowsprit (5) was movable, it could be drawn into the bow in port, or extended when setting the headsails.

• The sail rig of a smack is shown in Figure 22. In its simplest form it resembles the basic sloop rig viz: large gaff sail (6) together with a single staysail (7), connected to the stay by hanks. In addition there could be a gaff topsail (8) and a flying jib (9), this headsail was connected at its lower end to an iron ring or *traveller* on the bowsprit and its upper end connected to the *halliard* – it was not connected by hanks to a stay.

• In fine weather with the wind astern, ie when the vessel was running before a wind, an additional square sail was set, called a *running square sail.*

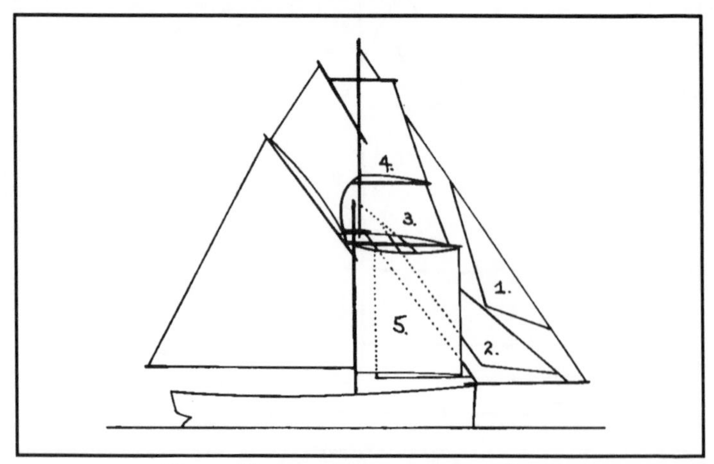

Figure 23. Smack fine weather sail rig.

• A distinct feature of a smack in port was its lightweight spar (10) half way down the mast, the large running square sail was connected to this spar. The spar was also called a *mainyard* spar, or *crossjack*, (crojack) spar. The spar was usually fixed athwart or transversely or sloping, or *cockabill*, when not in use. At the lower mast head is the rigging spreader (11).

Figure 23 shows a smack with its extra fine weather sails consisting of:

a) *headsails*: an outer flying jib (1) in addition to an inner flying jib (2).
b) *squaresails*: lower topsail (3), upper topsail (4), these square sails are connected along the length of the yard, as compared to the running square sail (5), which is connected at the yard arms and centre of the yard. Normally a single square topsail would be set, instead of the double square topsail.

• Steering was by means of a tiller.

• Usage was mainly in short duration fast passages on the coast carrying stone, sand, gravel or coal-smaller smacks were used for fishing or as fish carriers.

In conclusion: it is evident that the smack could have been an improved version of the sloop but despite increased tonnage and use of square sails and extra headsails, it was unable to attain the speed of the cargoless revenue sloops with their light displacement.

Displacement

Displacement is the weight, or mass, of water which a vessel displaces when floating (1) and is equal to the weight of the vessel loaded or unloaded, this is shown in Figure 24. The *draught*, or *draft*, (2) is the depth of water which the vessel draws, or sinks to, when afloat loaded or unloaded. Numbered draught marks are painted on the vessel stern and stem. Some vessels are shallow draught requiring less water depth than deep draught vessels.

The *waterline* (4) is the line made by the water surface on the floating vessels hull, loaded or unloaded.

The distance between the waterline and the upper deck level (5) is called the *freeboard* (3) as shown in the Figure 24.

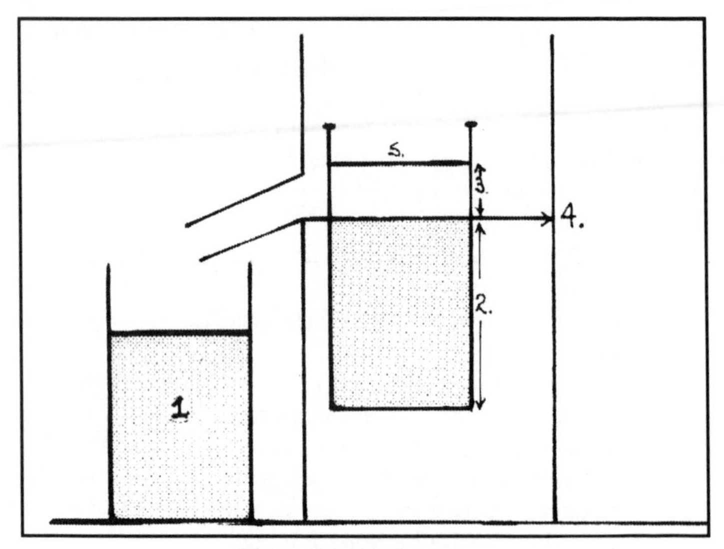

Figure 24. Displacement.

Revenue sloops would have a smaller displacement than cargo carrying sloops and smacks, the latter drawing more water when loaded.

Warships, which do not carry cargo, are measured in terms of *displacement tonnage*, being the actual weight, or mass, of the vessel including everything on board, guns, stores etc.

Tonnage

Tunnage of merchant vessels based on the capacity of French wine casks, previously described on page 33, was replaced by *tonnage* in the late 1780s when all vessels over 15 tons were registered in Lloyds Register of Merchant Shipping. This *register* includes other details of a merchant vessels *specification;* dimensions, tonnage, builder, owner, master, port of registry etc.

Dimensions of the cargo hold and details of a wooden sailing vessels structure are shown in the Figure 25. The main measurement in determining tonnage capacity are: hold length (1) and hold depth (2).

The hull *framework* consists of the keel (3) and keelson (4),

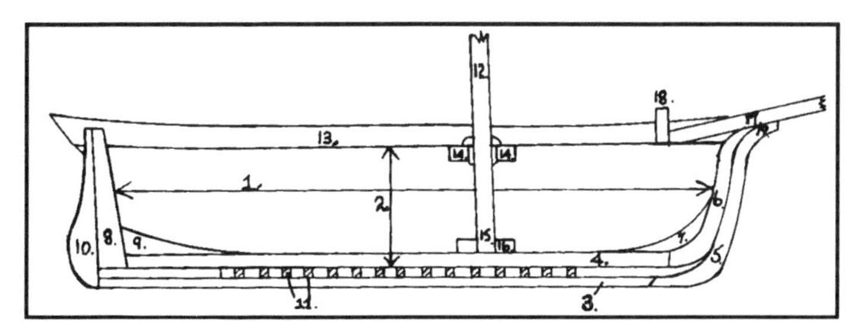

Figure 25. Hull longitudinal structure.

connected to the stem post (5) with its *apron* (6) and *knee* (7). See Plates 1, 2, 4 and 5. The head of the stempost has a knee-known by shipwrights as the "knee of the head" (19), this partly supports the bowsprit it is also where the figurehead is fixed. See Figure 61.

The stern post (8) and its *deadwood* (9) support the rudder (10). The transverse timbers, frames, or ribs (11) connect with the keelson and keel. See Plates 3 and 8.

• *Registered tonnage* is the tonnage entered in the Lloyds Register, this was measured according to different formulae for finding the vessels *volume* or cubical capacity which was converted in tons weight or mass.

• *Gross tonnage:* was based on the total volume of enclosed space in the vessels hull.

• *Net or nett tonnage:* is the vessels gross tonnage *less* the nonearning, or noncargo spaces; the accommodation space, engine room space, and water ballast space. This net tonnage value was carved into the *main beam* of the hold of wooden sailing vessels and was the basis on which port dues were calculated. Many small wooden sailing vessels did not have noncargo spaces and the gross tonnage equalled the net tonnage.

Under deck tonnage: is the gross tonnage or volume of enclosed space under the upper deck.

The entries for vessel tonnage in *Hen Longau Sir Gaernarfon* are net tonnage.

9. CUTTERS

Cutters were known to have existed from the early 1700s and had many different usages. Apart from Naval cutters, they found use as pilot cutters, fishing cutters and as recreational yachts. Not more than a dozen cutters are recorded in *HLSG* as being built in Caernarfonshire during 1750 to 1910, the majority were built between 1784 to 1830 – the sloop building period – and very few were built during 1830-1910. A large number of fishing cutters called *nobbies* were built in this latter period but being under 15 ton were not registered. Consequently information concerning Caernarfonshire cutters is based partly on the fishing cutter or *nobby* shown in Plates 42, 43 and 44. The navigation act of 1784 discouraged construction of vessels with L/B ratios greater than **3.5** evidently this had an effect on the building of fine lined vessels such as cutters, later this restriction was abolished in 1833.

The characteristic features of the smaller type of cutter shown in Figure 26 are summarised as follows:

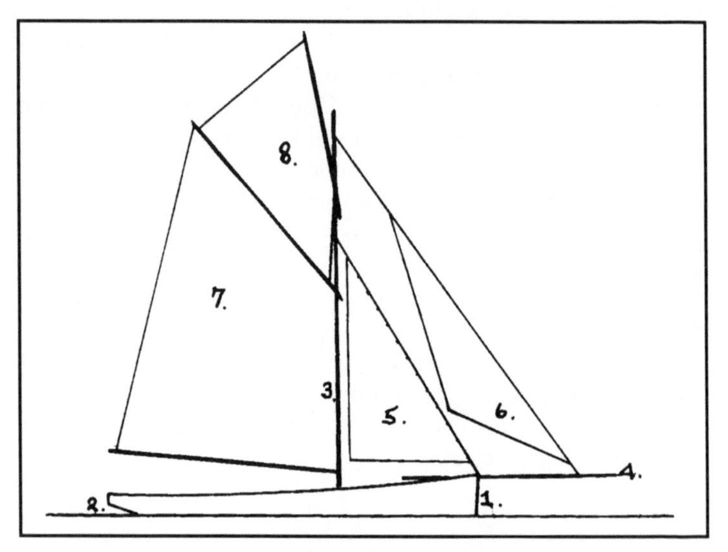

Figure 26. Small cutter-nobby rig.

• The dimensions of large registered cutters was approximately: 69ft (21m) length x 23ft (7m) breadth x 9.9ft (3.03m) depth. A length/breadth ratio of 3.0, and breadth /depth ratio of 2.3. The smaller fishing cutters had an average dimension of 37ft length x 10.5ft (3.2m) breadth and 6.1ft (1.9m) depth, indicating a L/B ratio = 3.5 and a B/D ratio = 1.72. These ratios indicate a relatively deeper and narrower hull than found in sloops and smacks.

• The large cutters had a tonnage between 90 and 200 ton, whilst the smaller cutters ranged in tonnage between 5 and 35 ton with an approximate average of 18ton.

• The hull form was a prominent characteristic of a cutter, see Plates 9, 10, 11, 12 and 13, it embodied the hull features of the caravel, which first appeared on the Caernarfonshire coast in the 1460s. Generally the hull had fine lines and was relatively beamy and sat deep in the water with a low freeboard, see Plates 42 and 44. It also had a steep deadrise and needed a deep water mooring, otherwise it heeled over on taking the ground unless supported by legs or props.

The carvel planked hull of larch or pitch pine on an oak skeleton framework gave the hull considerable strength. Earlier cutters had clinker hulls.

The *stem* was vertical or straight. The bow was sharp with a slight hollowing behind a vertical stem (1) which cut the water-hence giving the vessel its name as a *water cutter*, see Plate 12. The stern was either square with a transom in large cutters, or rounded with a counter (2), an extension of the hull beyond the stern post, see Plate 13.

• Decking covered the vessel completely, or was partial with an open *cockpit* typical of the fishing cutters, pilot cutters and yachts, see Plates 9, 10, 11 and 44. In the revenue cutters the bulwarks were high, but reduced to a low *coaming rail* in smaller cutters. Small cutters, had a focsle accommodation with a bogey stove. The nobby had an athwartship strengthening beam or thwart called a thoft-welsh *thoftia*, see Plate 43.

• The single mast (3) in the smaller cutters, Figure 26, was one part, see Plate 22. In the large cutters, Figure 27, it was two part: lower mast and topmast. The topmast could be lowered in some cutters. The mast was stepped into the keelson at a one third the deck length from stem. The mast was much taller than that of the smack and sloop.

• The bowsprit (4) was horizontal, movable or running, and could be reeved or run in when in port and run out when setting the jib which moved along the bowsprit on a iron ring, or *traveller*. The length of the bowsprit was 80% of the deck length in revenue cutters, and between 50-60% in smaller cutters. See Plates 21 and 43.

• The great sail area compared to hull size was another distinguishing feature of a cutter. It was of a much greater area than sloops and smacks.

a) *headsails*: included a staysail or foresail (5) connected by hanks to the forestay, which was fixed to the stem head and upto two flying jibs (6) connected to an iron traveller on the bowsprit.
b) *gaff sail*: included the large gaff sail (7) occupying 50% of the total sail area, together with a three or four sided gaff topsail (8).

The large revenue and smuggling cutters, Figure 27, set the following sails;

a) *headsails:* one staysail (1) inner flying jib (2) and outer flying jib (3). Flying jibs are not hanked to a stay.
b) *squaresails:* an upper topsail (4), a lower topsail (5) and a large deeply roached running square sail (6). The *roach* (7) is the curve in the sail foot.
c) *gaff sail:* a very large powerful gaff sail (8).

The great sail area required a large crew typical of revenue, naval and smuggling cutters to handle the sails.

• The cutters sailing performance outclassed other types of single masted wooden sailing vessels of the period, and was improved by means of a device called the *drop keel* used in certain kinds of cutter, particularly yachts.

If the sloop and smack were the "slow boats" – the cutter was most certainly the "speed boat" amongst single masted sailing vessels. The cutter, like the caravel, was a fast sailer and the forerunner of the *schooner*, a yachtlike vessel, which would dominate sail in Caernarfonshire from the 1850s.

• Smuggling was rife during the period 1810-1860 the success being due to the cutters being a match for the revenue cutters. Pilot cutters were based in ports to make speedy contact with incoming vessels. The fishing cutters, and nobbies, made speedy passages and this speed was also utilised in large trading cutters which carried perishable fruit from Spain and Portugal.

The web site "www. cimwch. com" – has a photographic collection of Caernarfonshire nobbies and other old sailing vessels.

Masting

Masts made of one piece from a single tree, usually Columbian pine, or douglas fir, are called *pole masts*, and are found in small sailing vessels, Plate 22. Larger masts are made up of several pieces joined or bound together by means of iron hoops, are called *made-masts*, or built-up masts, seen in early sailing vessels, carracks and barks. Rope lashings around a mast or spar are called *wooldings*.

• Figure 25 shows how the mast (12) is stepped. The mast heel (15) being fitted into the mast step (16) on the keelson (4). Bowsprits (17) have a heel abutting against the deck heel chock (18), Plate 43. The mast emerges through the upper deck (13) mast hole, Plate 11, and supporting mast partners (14). Wedges are driven in to produce a mast *rake* of

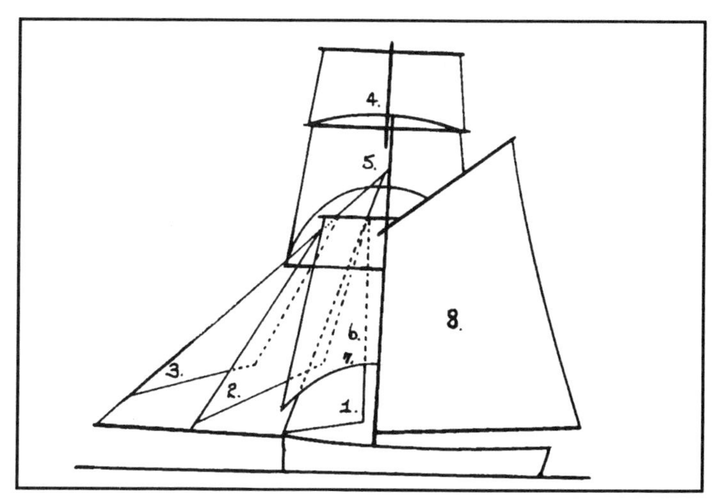

Figure 27. Large revenue cutter rig.

4 to 7 degrees from the vertical. The bowsprit can have a *steeving* varying from 2 to 30 degrees from the horizontal.

• *One part mast*: a pole mast, are found in small sailing vessels, Plate 22 and 25.

• *Two-part masts*: are composed of lower mast and upper topmast, and found in schooners, smacks, sloops, cutters and ketches.

• *Three-part masts:* consist of lower mast, topmast, and topgallant mast, are found in brigs, and full rigged ships. See Plate 32. Barques, brigantines, and barquentines have three part masts in addition to two-part masts. (Steel full-rigged ships may have two part masts-the lower mast and topmast being *combined,* with a separate topgallant mast above.)

• *Four-part masts:* consist of lower mast, topmast, topgallant mast and royal mast. The royal mast was equivalent to a flag pole, found in early barks.

The masts are named in order from the bow: foremast, mainmast, mizzen mast. These terms will be evident in descriptions of the fullrigged ship and other types of wooden sailing vessel described in later chapters.

Mast Head Assembly-Doubling

The component parts of a two, three or four part mast are joined together and supported in a masthead assembly or *doubling*. This involves binding and overlapping the parts amounting to 20-30% of the larger mast length as in Figure 28. The overlap or doubling occurs at the *masthead* (1) or upper end of a mast. See Plates 31 and 32.

The *top* is the name given to the lower mast head assembly in all square rigged vessels; brigantines, barquentines, barques and full rigged ships with three or four part mast. (See also page 119.)

In smaller vessels sloops, smacks, cutters, and schooners, which have a two part mast, it is called the "*crosstrees*", Figure 28 shows the "crosstrees", or masthead assembly, of a schooner, sloop, smack or cutter. The component parts of a small vessel mast head assembly are as follows:

• *Cheeks, or hounds* (2) – a ledge support for the trestle trees.

• *Trestle–trees* (3) are bars arranged in a fore and aft direction and fixed to the mast cheeks.

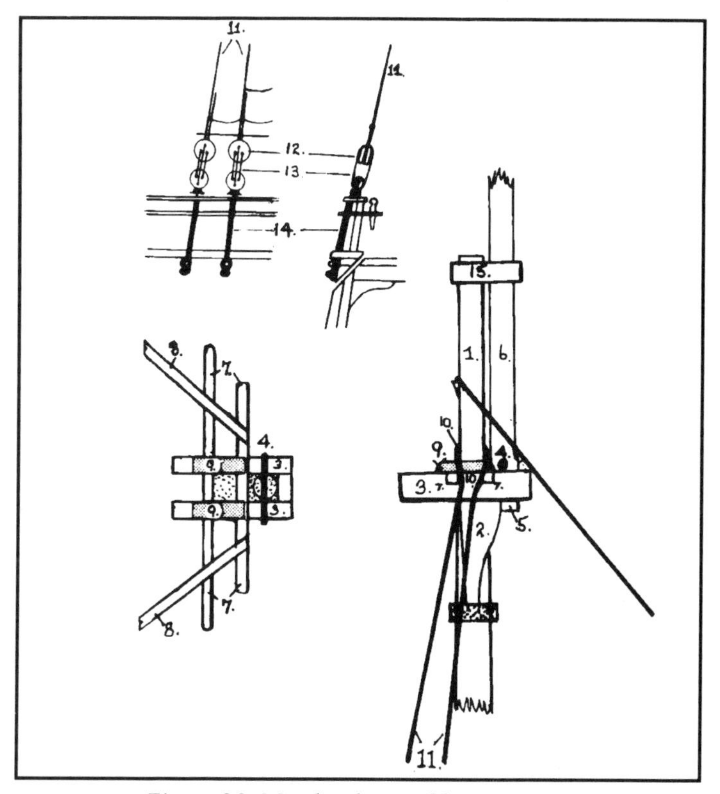

Figure 28. Masthead assembly structure.

- *Fids* (4) are iron or wood bars which pass through the topmast *heel* (5) and rest on the trestle-trees, to lock and support the topmast (6). *Fidding* is the removal of a fid allowing the topmast to be lowered using tackle – this happens to allow a sailing vessel to pass under a bridge.
- *Crosstrees* (7) are bars arranged athwartships to the trestle-trees to complete the mast head assembly framework, and to provide attachment for shrouds above if needed.
- *Spreaders* (8) adjust the tension of backstay rigging.
- *Cap* (15), this is a metal band connecting the head of a mast with the lower part of the mast above. The cap has a square opening on the head of the mast and a round opening allowing the topmast to slide through it when fidding.The cap strengthens the doubling.

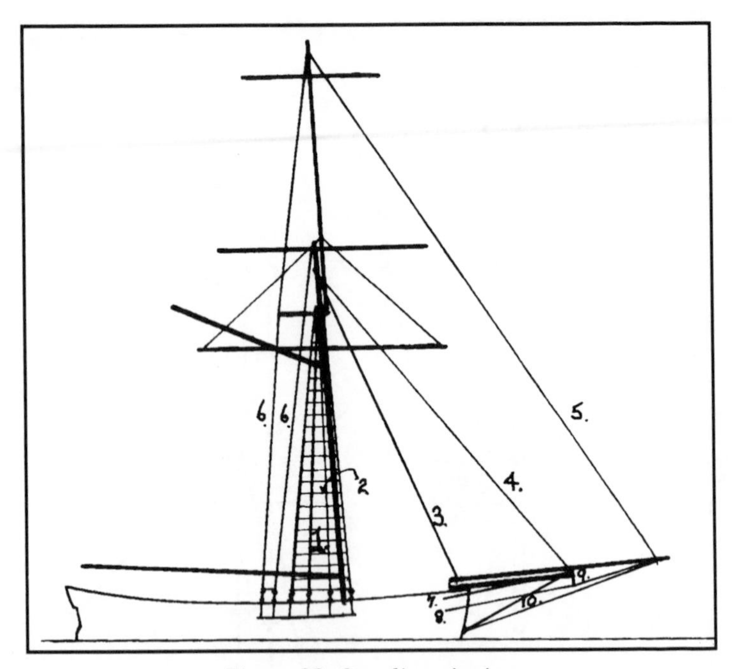

Figure 29. Standing rigging.

A bowsprit when fitted with a jib-boom may have a similar cap.

• *Bolsters* (9) prevent friction of the shroud rigging eyes (10) and provide a soft surface for the rigging to bend on.

The top, found in square rigged vessels, see Figure 48, is located *below* the "crosstrees" in a three or four part mast. See Plates 28 to 32.

Standing Rigging, see Plates 23 and 24

Standing rigging is the fixed rigging which provides support for the masts. It is made fast and not hauled in contrast to running rigging. It consists of hemp ropes or steel wire cable. Standing rigging consists of the following shown in Figures 28 and 29.

• *Shrouds* give a mast lateral support.

Figure 28 shows how the *shrouds* (11) are arranged in pairs, one end is fixed to a *dead eye* (12) and the line is looped as *rigging eyes* (10) around the masthead and over the bolster

(9) and returns to another deadeye. The deadeyes connect by *lanyards* (13), with other deadeyes fixed to the vessel side by means of *chainplates* (14), see Plate 23. *Riggging screws,* also called bottlescrews or turnbuckles, are an alternative to deadeyes and lanyards, see Plate 24.

• Figure 29 shows how the lower shrouds (1) connect the lower mast head with the vessel side. Topmast shrouds connect the topmast head with the *rim* of the top. Topgallant shrouds connect the topgallant mast head with the crosstree ends. Ratlines (2) are integral parts of the shrouds to climb the mast. See Plates 24, 28, 29 and 30.

• *Forestays* provide a mast with forward support: the *fore stay* (3) extends from the foremast head to the stem head, the *jib stay* (4) extends from the foremast head to the bowsprit; the *foretopmast* stay (5) extends from the foretop mast head to the jib–boom end. Stays are named according to the mast part they connect with. See Plates 30 and 33.

• *Backstays* (6) provide a mast with backward support and extend from the mastheads to the vessels sides were they are fixed via deadeyes, lanyards and chain plates as in Figure 28.

Bowsprit standing rigging, see Plate 60;

• *Shrouds* (7) and (8) similar to mast shrouds, provide sideways support, they are usually chains connecting with the bow head.

• *Martingale headstays* are tensioned by a short *martingale spar,* or dolphin striker (9) which acts like a mast spreader. In some vessels the spar may have its own standing rigging.

• *Bobstays* (10) are chains or ropes which pull the bowsprit downward to counteract the pull of the foremast stays, they connect with the stem.

• *Cutters:* the forestay connects with the stem head. The Bowsprit is long and moveable. The jib sails are set flying without hanks.

• *Sloop:* the forestay connects with the bowsprit nose. The bowsprit is short and fixed. The jib sails are set on stays with hanks.

Cymru a'r Môr articles relating to cutters:
"Swansea pilot cutters", W. Linnard, Vol11, 1987.

10. ONE-AND-A-HALF MAST VESSELS

Vessels having only one large *mainmast* and a smaller *mizzen–mast* form a class of vessel which has existed since about 1500; they arose from a common root and evolved into several different types which are called *ketches, galliots,* sailing barge *flats, dandy smacks* and *yawls*. The main common characteristic of this class of vessel is the possession of a *taller mainmast* near the bow and a *shorter mizzenmast* near the stern; – or are "one-and-a half mast" vessels! In addition, with exception of the yawls, these vessels had large cargo hatches.

The following is a brief survey of the different types of this class of vessel.

Galliot (Galleot-Galiot) Figure 30.

The galliot dates from about 1500 and originated in Holland and was a trading cargo carrier. Sir Francis Drake had a galliot in his expeditionary fleet to West Indies in 1585.

According to Appendix 2 *Hen Longau Sir Gaernarfon* – four galliots were built in Conwy from 1792 to 1805 and were sold away to Liverpool and Ireland, no more vessels of this type were built in Caernarfonshire, and maybe were the last of their type to be seen on this coast.

The following are some of the main characteristic features of a galliot;

• Dimensions of some typical vessels; a 71 ton galliot was of 58ft (17.8m) length x 17.4ft (5.4m) breadth x 8.6ft (2.65m) depth, another galliot was of 63.6ft (19.5m) length x 16.8ft (5.1m) breadth x 8ft (2.45m) depth. The length/breadth ratios = 3.3 to 3.7, indicating vessels narrower than sloops and smacks, with breadth to depth ratios of 2.0 and 2.1, i. e. relatively deep cargo carriers.

• The heavily built hull had carvel laid planking, was stem ended, or double ended, and rounded in section, flat bottomed, and similar to a barge (see-sailing flats). The hull had a distinct curve or *sheerline* to its upper edge (1). The bows (2) were bluff or rounded. *Leeboards* were fitted outside

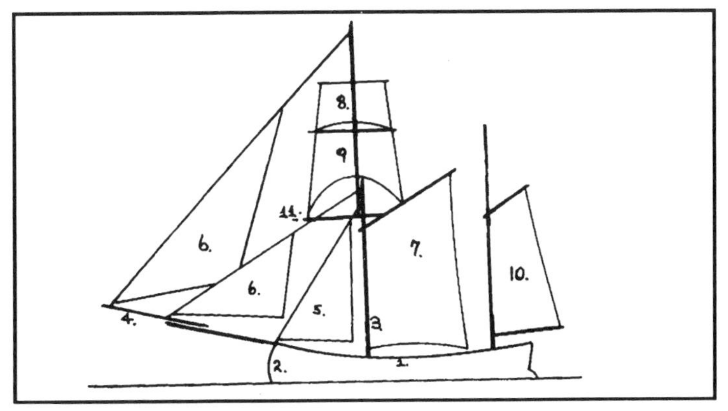

Figure 30. A galliot rig.

the hull as in most Dutch vessels and prevented the vessel drifting to leeward when underway when close-hauled.

Figure 30 shows a typical galliot with its tall *mainmast* (3). (Note: it is not called a foremast). Most galliots had a two part mast, lower mainmast and upper topmast, which was very bendy, being pulled forward by the forestay. Some galliots had a one part pole mast. The shorter mizzen single pole mast was stepped far aft.

• The bowsprit had a jib-boom (4) with a combined length of 80% of the hull or deck length

The sail rig is arranged as follows;

a) *headsails:* one staysail (5) hanked to the stay, together with one or two flying jib sails (6) on traveller irons connected to the bowsprit.

b) *gaffsail*: mainmast had one large *loose footed* gaff sail (7) without a boom, some had a boom; the *gaff spar* was usually fixed, or standing-not lowerable. The mizzen gaff sail (10) was similar but had a sail area 50% that of the main sail.

c) *square sails* included an upper topsail (8) a lower topsail (9), and a running square mainsail that would be set on the crossjack yard (11) in fair weather, both the latter were deeply roached having a deep curvature to the foot to be clear of the stays. The Frontispiece vessel 4, could be either a galliot or ketch, both vessels in early times had two topsails.

Ketch, Plates 49, 50 and 51.
Four ketches were built in Caernarfonshire in 1881 to 1891, almost 80 years after the building of the galliot, which poses a question why there was the need for this type of vessel at a time when the building of wooden sailing vessels was drawing to a close. The ketch had been in existence since the early 1600s as naval vessels, in later years it was used mainly as a cargo carrier in the coastal trade Plates 49, 51 and some traded to Spain, Mediterranean and crossed the Atlantic to Newfoundland. Smaller ketches were used in fishing.

The main characteristic features of the ketch, Figure 31, are summarised as follows:

• The average dimensions of a ketch; length 70.4ft (21.6m) x 20.5ft (6.3m) breadth x 9ft (2.7m) depth. The length/breadth ratio = 3.4 indicates a narrower vessel than the sloops and smacks, and similar to the galliot. The breadth /depth ratio = 2.2 indicates a vessel with depth as a cargo carrier, similar to the galliot.

• The length ranged from 30ft (9.2m) to 90ft (27.6m).

• Tonnage averaged 73 ton, and ranged from 30 to 150ton.

Ketches were also called smacks, but in general the ketch was twice as big as a smack, see Plate 49.

• The hull had fine lines, with a sharp bow and straight stem (1). The stern (2) could be either square with a transom, or rounded with a counter. Accommodation was either in the focsle or aft in the cabin below deck.

• The main mast (3) was two part composed of lower mast and the topmast (4), as in the galliot it was *bendy*. "Crosstrees" were between the mast part doublings.

The mizzen mast (5) was a single pole mast. See Plate 51. In the early naval bomb ketches the mainmast was stepped back 50% the deck length away from the bow to produce a large area of deck forward sufficient for a large gun. See Plate 37.

The bowsprit in trading ketches was fixed or standing, and lengthened by a tapering jib-boom. Fishing ketches had a running or movable bowsprit.

• The sail rig of the early 1600s ketch included square sails on the mainmast and the mizzen, in this respect it was

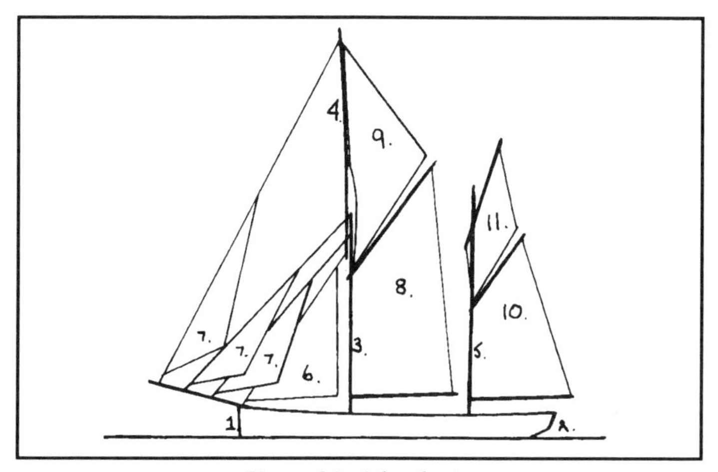

Figure 31. A ketch rig.

a similar sail rig to the galliot with its square sails, see the Frontispiece vessel 4. By the 1800s the square sails had disappeared, to be replaced by gaff topsails, to form the standard sail rig of all ketch rigs shown in the Figure 31, which continues to the present time in yachts and other pleasure vessels. See Plate 50.

The ketch sail rig comprises:

a) *headsails*: one staysail (6), and one to three jib sails (7).

b) *gaff sails*: include a gaff sail (8) and gaff topsail (9); and mizzen gaff sail (10) with mizzen gaff topsail (11). The mizzen gaff sail having a sail area about 50% of the gaff sail. (See Figure 40, showing different kinds of gaff topsails.)

• Steering in the larger ketches was by a steering wheel, behind which was a locker or wc; or by means of a tiller in smaller ketches.

Dandy Smack, Plate 48

The term *dandy* is used in different ways; by fisherman for a small fishing ketch; or for a small two masted schooner. The French use the term *dundee* for a ketch. In the Isle of Man the local fishing boat with "one-and-a-half" masts is called a Manx *dandy smack*.

David Thomas in *Hen Longau Sir Gaernarfon* records that

two wooden sailing vessels named as *dandy* were built in Caernarfonshire about 1870s; evidently this term is nearer to the Manx term dandy smack and could be identical. The following summarises the characteristic of a dandy smack:

- Dimensions: are difficult to obtain as most local dandy smacks could have been below 15 ton and not registered; the two vessels listed in *HLSG* are of a tonnage of 22 and 48 ton.

Dimensions of a 54 ton dandy smack are: 56ft (17.2m) length x 14.8ft (4.5m) breadth x 8.2ft (2.5m) depth. The length/breadth ratio = 3.7 indicating a narrow vessel and the breadth/depth = 1.8 indicates a deep hull.

- The hull is heavily constructed with carvel laid planking, the round hull indicates the need for a deepwater mooring. The hull, shown in Figure 32, and Plate 48 is *stem ended* (double ended) with straight stem (1) with the tiller controlled rudder hung on a straight stern (2). Some dandy smacks had a rounded stern with counter. A deck extends from bow to stern and the bulwarks are low. A large hatch opens into a capacious hold in cargo carrying dandy smacks.
- The masting consists of a tall single pole main mast (3), stepped further forward than in a ketch; the mizzen mast (4) is shorter and stepped very near the stern.

The bowsprit (5) is horizontal and measures 30 to 50% the deck length. An outrigger (6) is positioned at the stern to oneside of the tiller head and has a length similar to the bowsprit.

- Sail rig shown in Figure 32 consists of:

a) *headsails*: one hanked staysail (7), and one flying jib sail (8).

b) *main mast*: has a gaff sail (9) together with a four sided gaff top sail (10). (In the Plate 48, the gaff sail of the foreground dandy smack is lowered.)

c) *mizzen mast*: has a *lug* sail (11) bent to a hoisting lug yard (12) connected to the mast by an iron ring traveller. The four sided lug sail is connected at the foot to the outrigger. (In Plate 48 the mizzen lug sail is set.) The sail area of the mizzen lugsail is 33% that of the mainsail. The possession of a mizzen *lug* sail is the distinguishing feature of the dandy smack-placing it apart from the sail rig of a ketch or galliot.

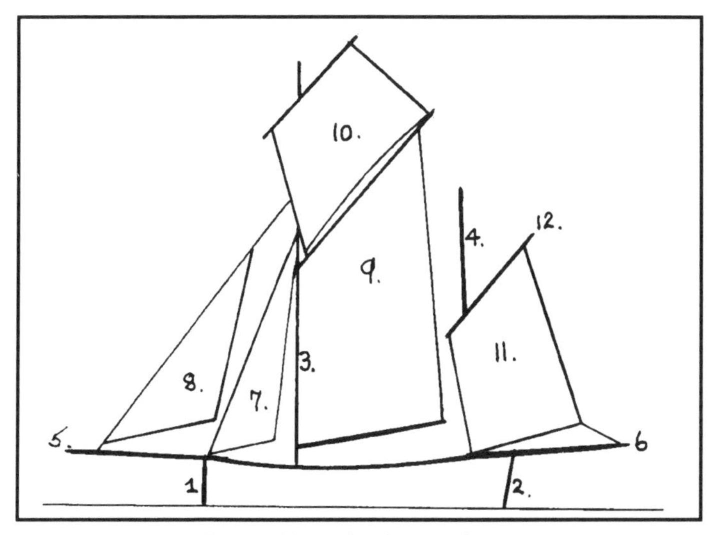

Figure 32. A dandy smack rig.

• The main usage of dandy smacks was for fishing and short distance cargo carriage on the coast. The Frontispiece vessel 5 shows a small fishing boat, possibly a small dandy smack.

Yawls

The *yawls or luggers,* see Figure 33, were found as beach craft in Anglesey during the 1850s. They resembled the dandy smack, being one-and-a-half mast vessels, but the masts were rigged with a large *lug* main sail (1) and a smaller *lug* mizzen sail (2).

The area of the mizzen lug sail was 25% that of the lug mainsail. The yawl was a fine lined, clincher built, stem ended (double ended), narrow vessel, between 20ft (6m) and 25ft (7.6m) in length and needed several men to row this open, undecked boat, and apart from fishing was used as a pilot boat.

The Manx nickie and Manx nobby were types of lugger yawls. Plate 46 shows a typical Manx nobby rebuilt at Waterside Marine boatyard Porth Penrhyn.

The Manx nobby Plate 46 differed mainly from the earlier Manx nickie in the following feature; it had a running or

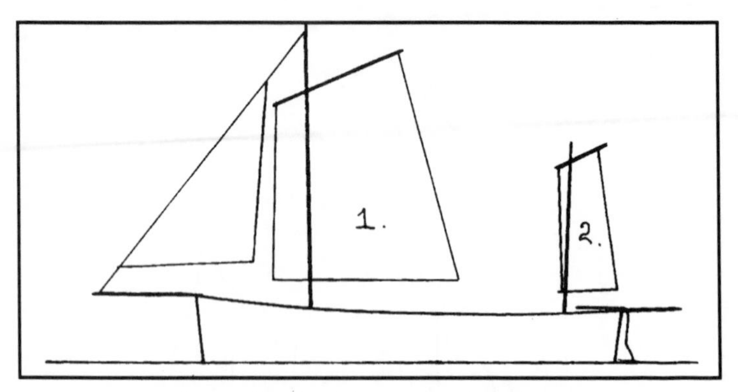

Figure 33. Yawl lugger beachcraft rig.

moveable bowsprit, with two headsails, whilst the Manx nickie Plate 47 was without, and had a dipping lugsail. The Manx nobby had standing lugsails.

Sailing Flats, Plate 51.

Sailing flats as the name suggests had flat bottomed hulls, and were also known as sailing barges. Basically they were canal boats, barges or lighters, with or without any sailing rig and were used originally on canals, rivers estuaries and in docklands, and were also known as "inside" flats. Those which were sail rigged and engaged in trading to northern Wales, and Lancashire were called "outside" flats and were one-and-a half masted vessels, see Plate 51.

Four vessels, called flats, were built in Conwy during 1802 to 1847, it is possible many more were built under 15 ton but were not registered. No detail is given in the Appendix 2, *HLSG*, as to the sail rig if any, and the following summarises the general characteristics of sailing flats and in particular the "outside" coasting flats:

- Tonnage ranged from 21 to 65 ton.
- The hull length averaged 60ft (18.4m) length x 12ft (3.7m) breadth for canal boats, and larger vessels measured 68ft (21m) length x 16.9ft (5.2m) breadth. The larger "outside" sailing flats were about 80ft (25m) length x 20ft (6.1m) breadth and were too big for most canal locks.

The hull was very narrow with length/breadth ratios between 3.9 and 5.0, and breadth to depth ratios 2.5 to 3.7

indicating *shallow* vessels. The flat bottom had hardly any deadrise and the vessels took the ground remaining upright.

Most hulls were stem ended-double ended, with bluff bows and sterns. A square transom was present in older flats. The bulwarks were absent or very low on "inside" flats, and in the form of an open rail in "outside" sailing flats. Steering was by means of a very heavy and long tiller. There were narrow side gangways on either side of the large hatch. The crew of 2 or 3 lived in a small cabin below decks aft.

• Masting – the small sailing flats had a single, lowerable, pole mast, and no bowsprit. The larger "outside"

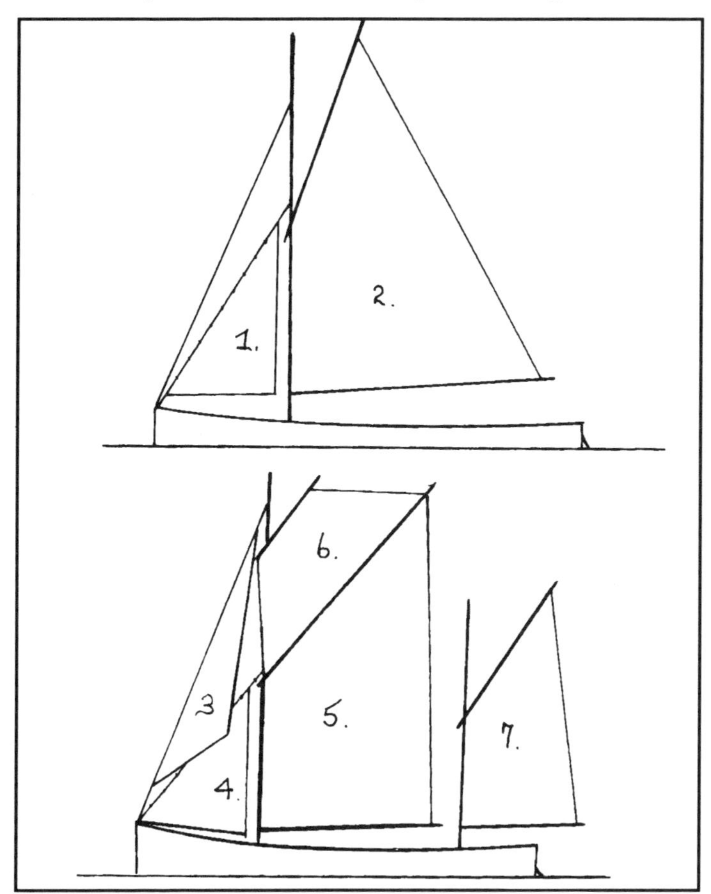

Figure 34. Mersey flats rig.

sailing flats had a tall single pole main mast, together with a shorter single pole mast aft, this was called a *jigger* mast. The "outside" flats were also called *jigger flats*. See Plate 51.

The sail rig for the two varieties of flats are shown in Figure 34.

a) The smaller sailing flat has a sloop rig composed of one hanked staysail (1) and a gaff sail (2).

b) The larger ketch rigged "outside" flat had a flying jib (3) and a hanked staysail (4), together with a gaff sail (5) and four-sided gaff topsail (6). The jigger mast was rigged with a gaff sail (7) with a sail area about half that of the main sail. When loaded and underway the flats had a very low freeboard.

Cargoes carried by the larger coastal flats include; slates, granite, limestone, sand and chemicals.

Summary and comparison of one-and-a-half-masted vessels:

Vessel	**Main mast**	**Mizzen mast**
Galliot	Gaff sail and square sails	Gaff sail
Ketch	Gaff sail and gaff topsail	Gaff sail and gaff topsail
Outside flat	Gaff sail and gaff topsail	Gaff sail only
Dandy smack	Gaff sail and gaff topsail	Lug sail
Yawl	Lug sail	Lug sail
Inside flat	Gaff sail	None

Survival

The lug sail is fitted to the lovely Trearddur Bay sailing dinghy Plate 45 produced at Classic Sailboats, Bethel to a design almost one hundred years old. The sail is a dipping lug somewhat resembling a gaff sail. The yard carrying the sail projects forwards of the mast and is lowered or dipped when the boat is going about and the rehoisted when back on the new tack. The hull is planked in spruce on elm ribs fastened by copper rivets.

Cymru a'r Môr article; "The Tenby Lugger", Anthony H Galvin, Volume 24, 2003.

11. FORE-AND-AFT SCHOONERS

Schooners are a class of sailing vessel that can be defined as having two or more masts each of near equal height and each mast rigged with fore and aft gaff sails and staysails; the masts can be with or without square topsails. The characteristic structural features of schooners are therefore;

- Two or more masts-some schooners have upto seven masts.
- Masts are of near equal height *without* tops.
- Sail rig is fore-and-aft; gaffsails and staysails.
- Square topsails may, or may not, be present.

Since the schooners are a large class of vessels there are different *variations* of the schooner which are as follows:

- Pole masted small schooners.
- Fore-and-aft large schooners, with two part masts.
- Topsail schooners with square topsails and two part masts.

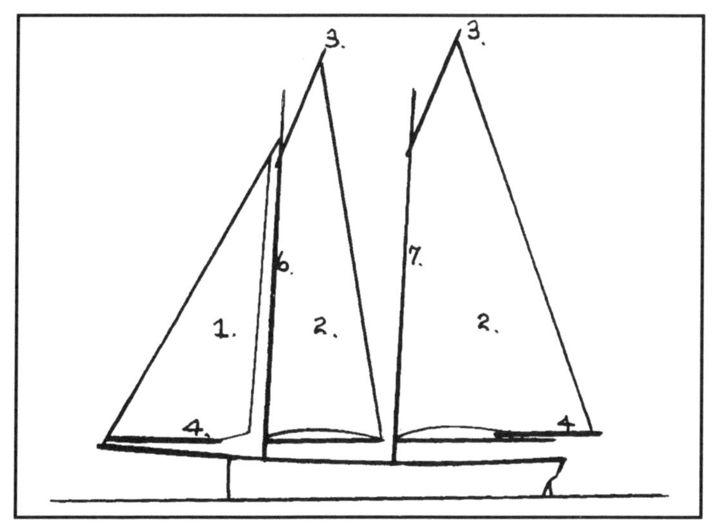

Figure 35. A shallop rig.

Pole Masted Small Schooners – Plate 52

These small sailing vessels have two pole masts of near equal height. The main types of two masted, pole mast schooners recorded in *Hen Longau Sir Gaernarfon* are called: *shallops* and *wherries*. They were in existence since the 1700s and used for fishing, yachting, pilotage, and smuggling in the Irish Sea, and are extinct but for a model of one shallop preserved in the Manx Nautical Museum at Castletown.

The following compares the main differences between the shallop and wherry:

- *Shallop*: see Figure 35 and Plate 52; the vessel has a near vertical *foremast* stepped 12.5% of the deck length from the stem, whilst the near vertical *mainmast* is stepped 50% of the deck length from the stem. Found in Caernarfonshire, Isle of Man and Cumberland.
- *Wherry*: see Figure 36; the vessel has a near vertical *foremast* stepped 25% of the deck length from the stem, whilst the raked *mainmast* at 15-20 degrees from vertical, is stepped 60% the deck length from the stem. Found in Caernarfonshire, Ireland and south Wales.

Only one shallop is recorded in *HLSG* as being built in Caernarfon in 1821, whereas 19 wherries are recorded for Caernarfonshire between 1786 and 1829. The shallop tonnage was 11 ton and wherry tonnage ranged between 5 to 19 ton. It is therefore possible that many more of these small

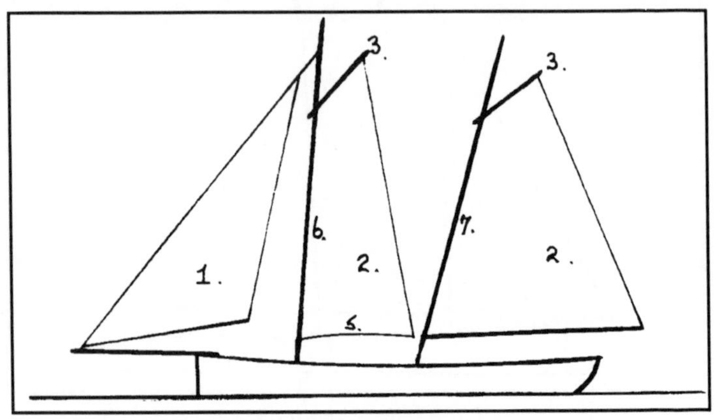

Figure 36. A wherry rig.

two masted schooners were built in Caernarfonshire and not registered due to their tonnage being less than 15 ton.

• Dimensions; shallop – 39.6ft (12.1m) length x 12.9ft (3.96m) breadth x 6ft (1.8m) beam. L/B = 3.06, B/D = 2.15 this indicates a normal beam and depth of hull.

Wherry – 30.5ft (9.36m) length x 10.8ft (3.3m) breadth x 4ft (1.22m) depth. L/B = 2.82, B/D = 2.7, relatively more beamy than a shallop

• Hull was light and fine lined, mainly clinker laid pine planks on an oak skeleton framework. Sharp stem, rounded hull with a deadrise. The stern was square with a transom Plates 3 and 6, or could be rounded.

Some were open boats with thwarts, and others partly decked or completely decked, see Plate 52.

• Sail rig was entirely fore-and-aft composed of staysail (1) to bowsprit, and gaff sails (2) on each mast, the gaff spars were short (3). The Manx shallop had *battens* (4) in the headsail foot, and also to extend the gaff sail boom. The wherry fore gaff sail was loose footed or without a boom (5).

• The masts were named *foremast* (6) and *mainmast* (7) and were without any standing mast rigging. The bowsprit was long and upto 50% the deck length. To avoid seizure for smuggling, which flourished at this time, the bowsprit had to be standing, without a traveller for a flying jib, and not clincher built – this Act was cancelled in 1833.

As the small two masted pole schooners were fast sailers they found usage in fishing, fish carriers, pilotage, ferries, recreational yachts, cargo carriage, and smuggling.

Fore-and-aft Schooners

Fore-and-aft schooners are those sailing vessels which have two or more masts, of near equal height, each mast composed of two parts, with fore-and-aft gaff sails and stay sails to each mast. They are *without* square topsails, and include the usual headsails.

The records in *Hen Longau Sir Gaernarfon* do not distinguish between the different variety of schooner built other than record them as either two masted or three masted schooners. Consequently it is not known whether the fore-and-aft type schooner was ever built in Caernarfonshire.

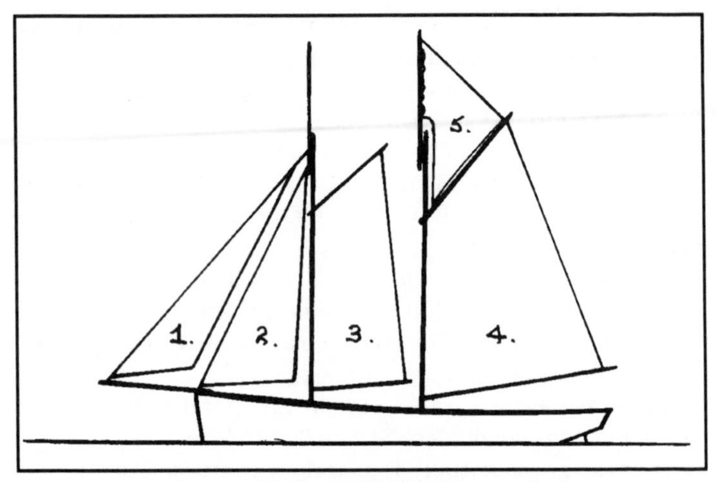

Figure 37. Fore-and-aft schooner rig.

The Figure 37 shows a typical fore-and-aft schooner, this type of schooner was rare in Britain but much more common in North America. The schooner shown was used as a pilot boat on the Mersey and would have been a frequent visitor off the north Wales coast to *Point Eilianus (Lynas)* picking up and dropping the pilots from the busy Mersey shipping. In addition they may have been used as recreational yachts in Caernarfonshire.

- Dimensions: 74ft (23m) length x 18ft (5.5m) breadth x 10ft (3.07m) depth. L/B = 4.1 B/D = 1.8, this indicates a narrow and deep hull. The tonnage was 116 ton, the tonnage ranged between 120-200 tons.

A summary of hull structure is given in the chapter on topsail schooners.

The two masts were of near equal height and composed of two parts lower mast and topmast each part assembled by means of the doublings, "crosstrees", the masts being named the foremast and mainmast. The third mast is called the mizzen in three masted fore-and-aft schooners. Very large fore-and-aft schooners with upto seven masts were found in North America had masts named: *fore, main, mizzen, jigger, spanker, driver and pusher*.

- The sail rig to each mast was fore-and-aft with a gaff

sail and staysail in addition there could be a gaff topsail, together with the usual headsails to the bowsprit.

The names of the sails in the Figure 37 are as follows:

(a) *headsails*: jib sail (1), and foremast staysail (2).

(b) *gaffsails:* gaff foresail (3), gaff mainsail (4) and mainmast gaff topsail (5).

Sail Parts & Running Rigging

Staysails or three sided sails: include the mast staysails, and headsails or the jibs. The staysails are named according to the mast part the stay connects with e.g.: topmast staysail, topgallant staysail and royal staysail.

• Figure 38 shows a typical three-sided sail and its rigging. Each sail is composed of canvas cloths sewn together and bound by a rope sewn around the edge called the *boltrope.*

• The *head* (1) is the top corner of the sail. *Leech* (2) is the vertical edge. *Luff* (3) is sail edge connecting to the stay by means of hanks. See Plate 30. *Foot* (4) is the sail lower edge. *Tack* (5) is the sails forward lower corner. *Clew* (6) is the sails after lower corner. *Cringles* (7) are loops or rings in the sails

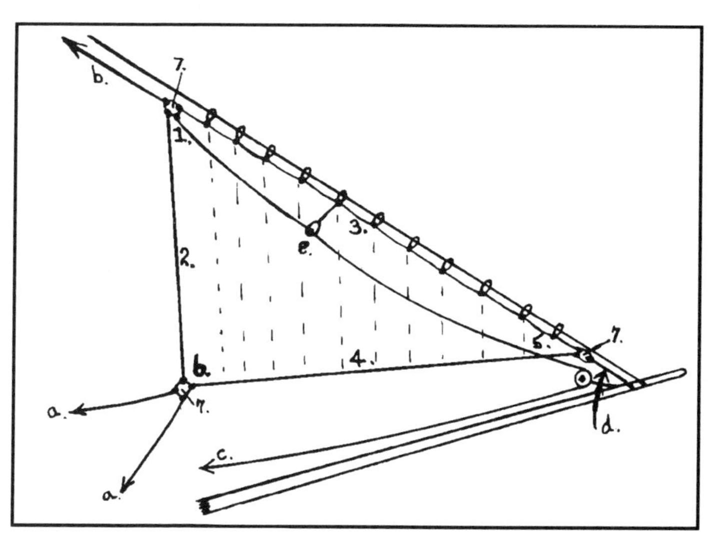

Figure 38. Staysail and running rigging.

boltrope Plate 33.

• Staysail running rigging is shown in Figure 38 and Plate 33, and consists of; *sheets* (a) connected to the sail clew; *halliards* (b) which hoist the sail; *downhauls* (c) which haul down the sail to the bowsprit during furling; Plate 26. the *lizard* (e) is a fairlead allowing the downhaul to run freely. The *tack* (d) connects the sail corner with the bowsprit.

Gaff sails or foursided sails, connect to the mast (4), gaff spar (5) and gaff sail boom (6), see Figure 40.

• *Boom* is the lower horizontal spar connecting with the mast through either wooden *jaws* and a *parall* or an iron *gooseneck*, universal joint.

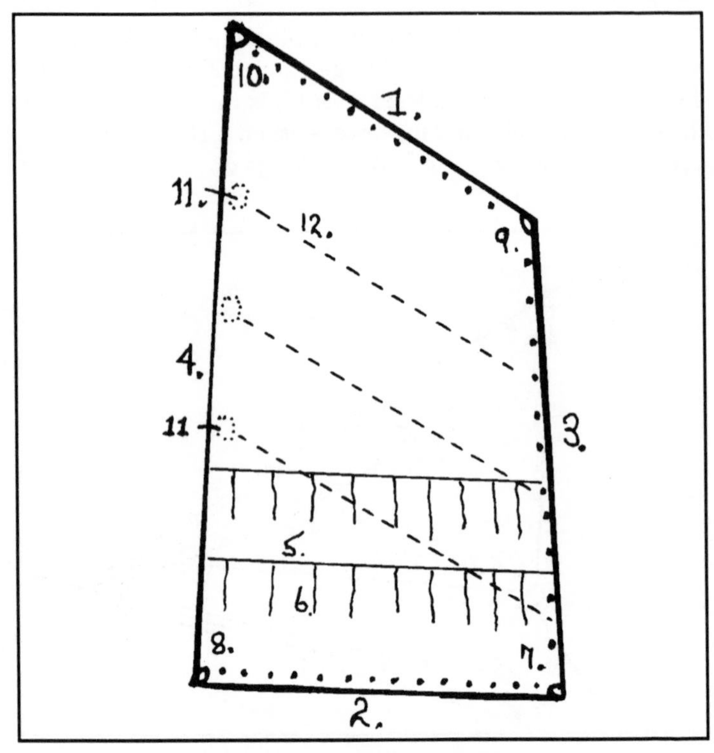

Figure 39. Gaff sail structure.

- *Gaff spars* are of two kinds:

(a) *hoisting* gaff with wooden jaws and parral, the gaff spar is raised or lowered by *halliards*. Found in small sailing vessels, schooners etc. See Plate 27.

(b) *standing* gaff is fixed by a gooseneck to the mast by which the gaff spar remains aloft permanently. Found in the large sailing vessels, barques etc.

Hoisting gaff sail parts & running rigging: Figure 39 and Plate 32.

Head (1) of gaff sail connects with the gaff spar by means of *seizings* of lacing, or *robands* or rope bands. *Foot* (2) of gaff sail connects with the boom by means of lacing. Some gaff sails are loose-footed, without a boom. *Luff* (3) of sail connects with mast by means of lacing or wooden *hoops*. *Leech* (4) is the free edge of the sail. See Plates 27 and 32.

Reefing band (5) is a strip of canvas connecting with the *reef point lines* (6). They are found only on the hoisting gaffsail and are used to reduce the sail area.

Clew (8) is the after lower corner and the *tack* (7) is the forward lower corner securing the sail to the boom.

Throat (9) the inner top corner of the sail. *Peak* (10) is the upper after corner of the gaff sail. Cringles are fitted into the sail head, clew, tack, peak, throat and reef.

The hoisting gaff sail is *furled* by lowering the gaff spar to the boom by means of the peak *halliards* and throat *halliards*.

When the gaff sail is set the gaff spar is steadied by *vangs*, and the gaff sail boom steadied by *boom guys* and *boom topping lifts*.

Standing gaff sail parts & running rigging: (1) *head* connects to the standing gaff spar by either hoops or a track; (2) *foot* connects to the boom by a track or is loose footed; (3) *luff* is connected by seizings or robands to an *iron jackstay* on the mast. The remaining parts are similar to the hoisting gaff sail as in Figure 39.

The standing gaff sail is *furled* by means of *brail ropes* connecting with the sail leech, they pass through *brail holes* (11) and hence by means of the *brail leads* (12) passing through the mast *brail blocks* and down to the deck. The sail is then gathered towards the mast. The sail head and foot are

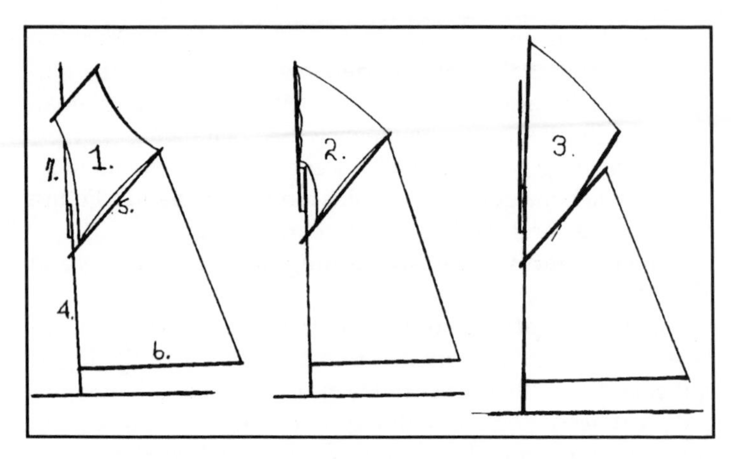

Figure 40. Different gaff topsails.

hauled by *outhauls* and *inhauls*.

The gaff spar and boom are supported at their ends by *wire spans*.

The boom guys steady the boom.

(Peak and throat halliards are not found on the standing gaff.)

After the sail is furled it is bound to the gaff spar, boom

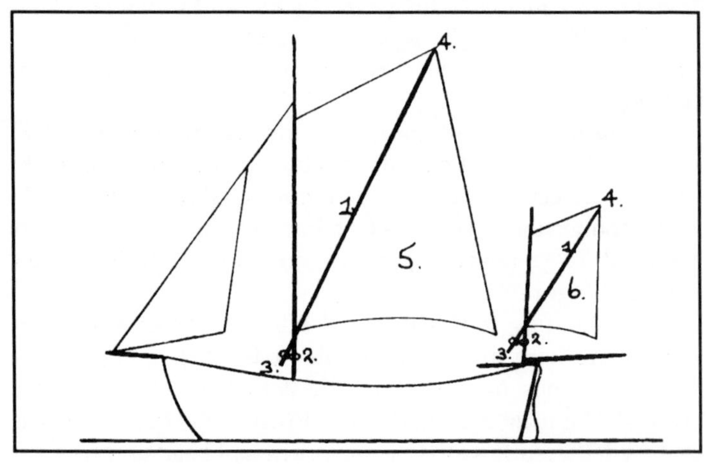

Figure 41. Ynys Enlli beachcraft, fore-and-aft spritsail rig.

or mast, by means of short lengths of line called *gaskets.*

Gaff Topsails are either threesided, or foursided sails, connected to the topmast (7). Figure 40 shows the three kinds of gaff topsail namely; (1). *square* gaff topsail with four sides bent to a short topsail spar, (2). *jib-headed* gaff topsail with its roach near the masthead doubling, and (3) *jackyard* topsail laced to the jackyards.
(1) Square gaff topsails are seen in Figures; 18, 22, 23, 31, 32, and 34. Also Plate 47.
(2) Jibheaded gaff topsails are seen in Figures; 31, 37, 44, 45, 47, 51 and 52. Also Plates 56, 61, and 63.
(3) Jackyard gaff topsails are seen in Figure 26.

OTHER SAIL TYPES

Fore-and-aft Spritsail: Figure 41, this is a foursided, fore-and-aft sail, which is extended by means of a *sprit spar* (1) crossing the sail diagonally from a *snotter* (2), connecting with the sprit *heel* (3), and on to the *peak* (4) of the sail. No boom is present – the sail being loose-footed.

Ynys Enlli beach boats of the 1800s, were typical "one-and-a-half mast" class vessels, and set a mainmast spritsail (5) together with a small mizzen spritsail (6) as shown in Figure 41. (The *fore-and-aft* spritsail should be distinguished from the *bowsprit* sprit sail that was set on the *bowsprit* of galleons and other sailing vessels of the 1500s – Figures, 12, 13 and 14.)

Lateen sails, Figures 9, 10 and 11, were the sails of the caravel sailing vessel of the 1450s, the three sided sail had its luff bent, or connected, to the lateen yard hoisted obliquely to the mast, like a lug sail. Plates 46, 47 and 48. The lateen sail was the mizzen mast rig of early three masted sailing ships, it was then replaced by a fore-and-aft spritsail and finally by the gaff sail.

Trysail is the name given to a four sided, fore-and-aft sail, set to a boom and gaff spar, ie a gaff sail as in schooners – it is also synonymous for spankers, drivers, and spencers in other square riggged vessels. (Early gaff sails had a very short gaff spar making the sail appear triangular.)

Storm sail is a three sided sail set on the mizzen boom and mast of barques and full rig sailing ships. See Plates 71 and 72 it is equivalent to a gaff spar sail divided diagonally from throat to clew.

The sailing boat *bermuda* sail is three sided with a long luff.

Cymru a'r Môr, articles relating to fore-and -aft schooners include:
"Irish sea wherries, schooners or shallops", M. K. Stammers, Vol 13, 1990.
"Rescued near Ynys Enlli 1866", O. T. P. Roberts, Volume 20, 1999.

12. TOPSAIL SCHOONERS

Following the end of the French wars in 1815, the peak period of sloop building declined in the 1820s and 1830s, a time which also coincided with that of general industrial depression, see graph Figure 15, but despite this a spirit of optimism prevailed in the building of a new harbour in Porthmadog in 1824. The coronation of Queen Victoria in 1837 ushered in a period of renewed industrial activity, the products of which, particularly slates, called for a renewal of shipbuilding. Fast deepwater vessels were needed for overseas transport in international markets and the *topsail schooner* was the means to this end, consequently schooner building in Caernarfonshire reached a peak in 1840 as shown in the graph Figure 42, and the production was maintained until 1910 when a total of 483 schooners had been built.

The "Western Ocean", as the Atlantic was called by old seafarers, was part of the call of the sea which attracted young men from agricultural work during the depression in agriculture of the 1860s and 1870s.

Incompetency was a cause of ship loss and consequently the Navigation Act of 1850 introduced compulsory certification of Masters and Mates:

a) Master – "Fore-and-Aft" vessels only, for coastal and home trade.
b) Ordinary Master – "Square Rig" for any vessel fore-and-aft, square rig, deepsea and foreign-going.
c) Master "Steamships" for steamers foreign going.

The examination conducted in English was a handicap to thousands of young monoglot Welshman of Caernarfonshire who went to sea in vessels in which the shipboard language was English.

Schooners had existed since the early 1700s and became prevalent in Wales from the early 1800s onwards, see Frontispiece vessel **3**. Schooners were cheap to build and required fewer crew and met the need for deepwater cargo transport. The type of schooner built for this trade was firstly the *two masted* topsail schooner and much later during the

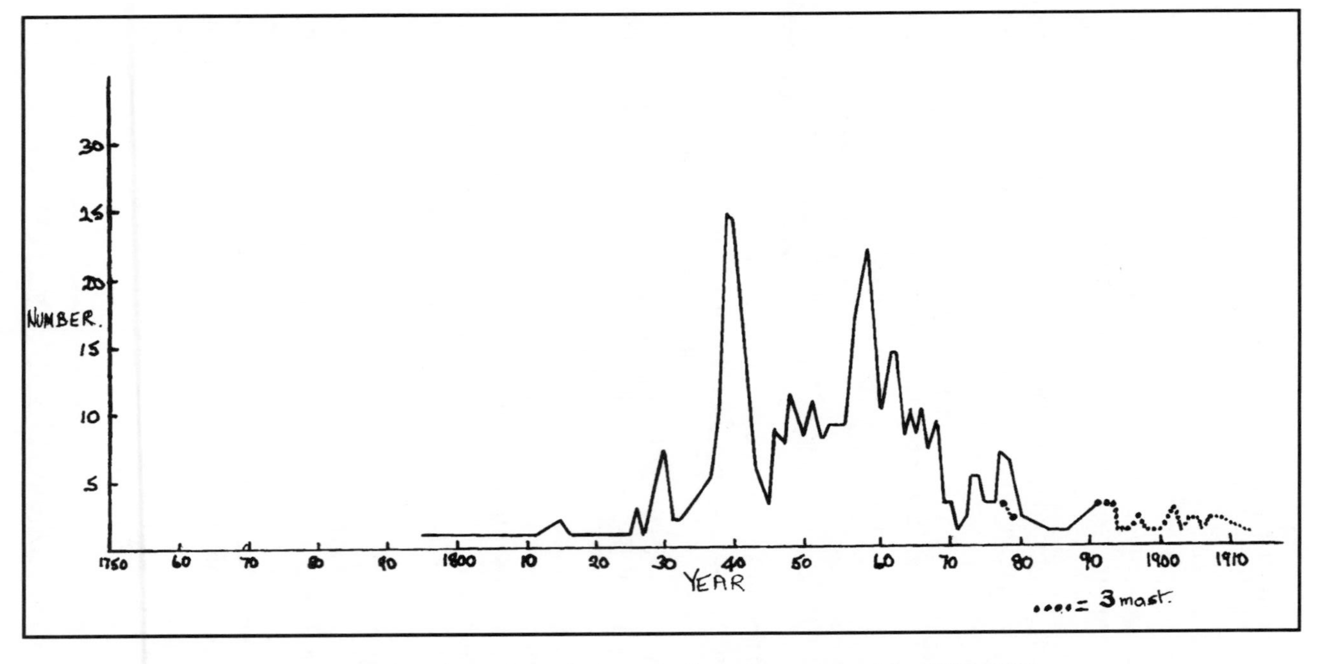

Figure 42. Total number schooners built in Caernarfonshire 1800-1910.

1890s – the *three masted* topsail schooner.

Appendix 2 of *Hen Longau Sir Gaernarfon* lists a total of 483 schooners built in Caernarfonshire during the period 1795 to 1913, of which 446 are listed as *two* masted schooners, and 37 as *three* masted schooners; see graph Figure 42.

Register of Caernarfonshire Sailing Vessel Pictures

Pictures, and models, of schooners and other sailing vessels existed in Caernarfonshire homes during the 1900s – and it is reasonable to expect that many of these schooner pictures still remain on walls or in attics as mementoes of former seafaring ancestors. The creation of a central register of these existing schooner pictures, and other types of sailing vessel, would be a valuable historical record of the maritime heritage of Caernarfonshire. Photographs, names and dates of the vessel could be sent to the Archives Office, Caernarfon. This would be a valuable addition to the existing collections already donated to Gwynedd Archives.

Two Masted Topsail Schooner Plates 51, 53, 54 and 55

The building of schooners was distributed in Caernarfonshire as follows: Porthmadog 32%, Pwllheli 17%, Nefyn 13%, Caernarfon 10%, Porth Dinllaen 9% with the remaining 9% distributed between Conwy, Caerhun, Trefriw, Bangor, Y Felinheli *(Port Dinorwig)*, Trefor and Borth-y-gest.

The importance of Porthmadog as a leading schooner building port is described in detail in: *Porthmadog Ships* Emrys Hughes and Aled Eames.

The following summarises the characteristic features of the two masted topsail schooner:

- Dimensions. A random selection of dimensions from a large sample showed vessel length ranged betwen 60ft (18.5m) and 87ft (26.7m); breadth ranged from 18.6ft (5.7m) to 28.1ft (8.6m), and depth ranged from 10.5ft (3.2m) to 14.6ft (4.4m).

Calculation of the average dimensions of a two masted topsail schooner gave the following value: 76ft (23.3m) length x 20.5ft (6.2m) breadth x 10.7ft (3.3m) depth.

The L/B ratio = 3.7 indicating a narrow hull, and the D/B ratio = 1.91 indicating a deep hull. Plate 51 shows the deep

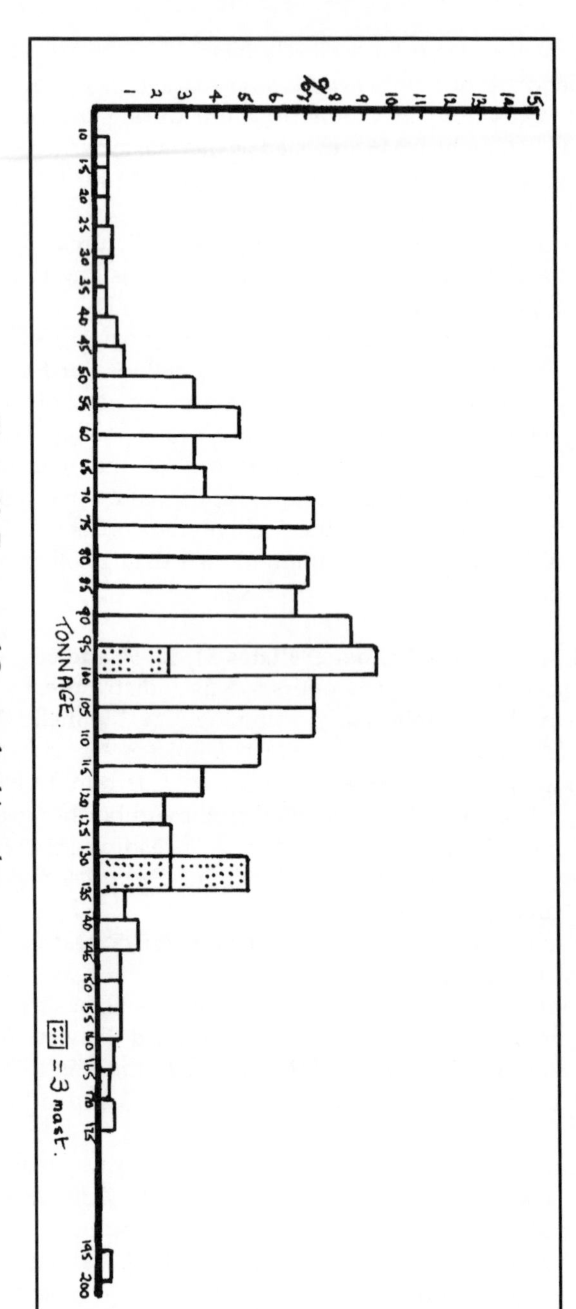

Figure 43. Tonnage of Caernarfonshire schooners.

nature of the two masted schooner hull compared to the ketch and flats.

• Tonnage distribution is shown in the graph Figure 43. The average tonnage is approximately 96 ton. The graph also shows about 10% of the total tonnage was less than 50 tons for some very small schooners which could have been open, or partly decked, shallop or wherry type vessels.

• The Caernarfonshire schooners were all built of pine planking, carvel laid on a skeleton framework of oak, much of the timber needed was imported. See Plates 14 and 15. Some iron and steel schooner hulls were built in Amlwch.

• The basic hull form resembled that of the cutter in having broad bows like a cods head and narrowing to the stern like a mackerels tail. The stem was sharp and straight with a slight rake; the stern was square with a long counter. Plates 12, 13 and 53. The hull had a graceful lengthwise curvature, or *sheer*, which raised the stem and bow allowing the schooner to mount and ride over rough seas. See Plate 54. Many schooners registered in *HLSG* were also built by conversion from large smacks and cutters.

• Masting of two mast topsail schooners, like many other wooden vessels, was mainly of Douglas fir, and the masts named from the bow as foremast and mainmast.

Each mast was two part composed of a lower mast and upper topmast, with doublings and "crosstrees" connecting both parts. See Figure 28. *(No top in schooners.)* Both masts were near equal height, but the mainmast could be slightly taller. The standing bowsprit was very highly steeved, or sloping at an angle to the horizon, see Plates 51, 53 and 57.

Small schooners which had pole masts only, and were without top masts, were called *bald-headed* schooners. See Plate 25 and 53.

Single topsail schooner. Plates 53 and 55.

• Sail Rig; Figure 44, shows a typical *single topsail* schooner with its basic fore-and-aft headsails, staysails, and gaff sails, together with the distinguishing characteristic square topsails. The sails are named from the bowsprit end:

a) *headsails:* flying jib (1), outer boom jib (2), standing jib (3) and forestaysail (4).

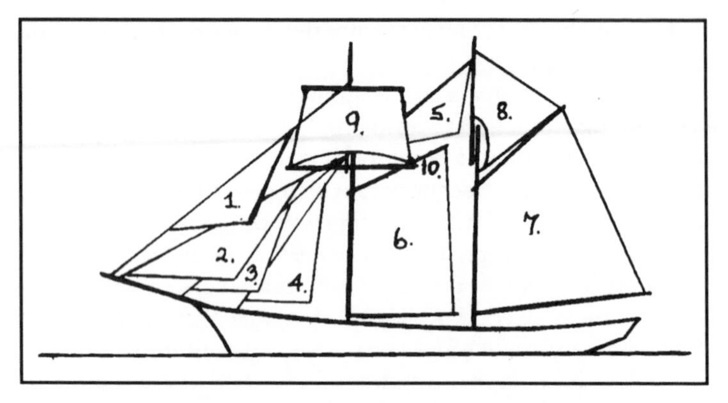

Figure 44. A two masted schooner, single topsail rig.

b) *mast staysail*: main topmast staysail (5).
c) *gaffsails:* gaff foresail (6); gaff mainsail (7) jib-headed gaff topsail (8).
d) *square sails:* fore topsail (9).

All schooners carried a fine weather *running square sail* connecting with the lower foreyard (10), by means of yard ropes and staysail halyards, seen also in sloops, cutters and ketches.

Double topsail schooner. Plate 54

The *double topsail* schooner shown in Figure 45, has two topsails on the fore topmast, named the fore lower topsail (9) and the fore upper topsail (10) – all other sails are named as for a *single* topmast schooner, Figure 44.

Early naval schooners in the 1780s could set single or double topsails on *both* masts.

• Usage: the two masted schooners had fast sailing ability and found use in carriage of perishable fruits and vegetables from Portugal and Spain, salt codfish, or dried stockfish from Newfoundland, in addition to being carriers of slate. Most of the early two masted topsail schooners were used in coastal work in the home trade and to Europe and a lesser extent transatlantic.

Amongst the noted *single* topsail schooners were those from Brittany that brought the onion sellers – "Shoni Winwns" – to Wales.

The early American single topsail schooners called Baltimore schooners, were fast sailing revenue and pirate schooners of the type shown in Plate 55.

Three Masted Topsail Schooner

During the 1870s shipbuilding declined to its lowest level in Caernarfonshire as shown in the graph Figure 42; at this time wooden sailing ships could be bought cheaply from North America, and in addition could be delivered with a cargo of softwood timber. The peak years for wooden shipbuilding had been passed in 1860 and the last wooden sailing vessels were built in Porth Dinllaen 1876; Pwllheli in 1878; Bangor in 1879 and Nefyn in 1880.

A period of financial depression prevailed. Despite this gloomy time *three* masted topsail schooners were being built, one in Pwllheli 1876, and one in Nefyn in 1877 – maybe as a last fling gesture before closing the shipyards. Meanwhile Porthmadog launched three, three-masted topsail schooners between 1877 and 1878, but gloom set in again in 1879 with the closure of Porthmadog shipyard from 1879 to 1884.

The Porthmadog shipyard reopened in 1885, see the Figure 46, with the building of three masted topsail schooners which came off the stocks steadily from 1891 until the final closure of the yard in 1913, with the launch of the

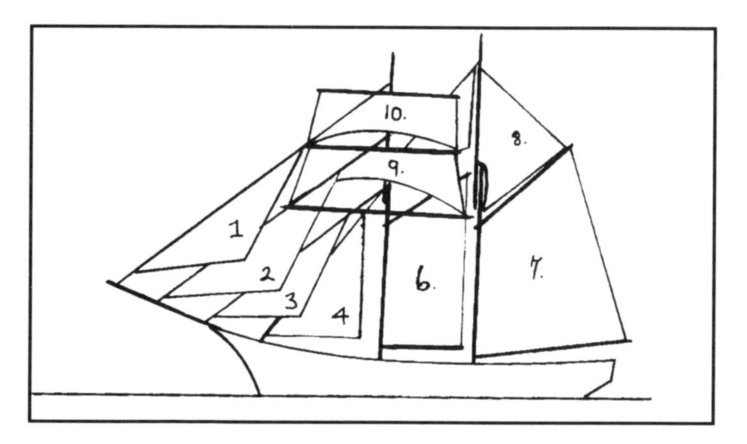

Figure 45. A two masted schooner, double topsail, rig.

last large wooden sailing vessel to be built in Caernarfonshire during the 20th century, namely the three-masted topsail schooner the *Gestiana.*

Porthmadog ship construction had reached the peak of perfection during these last 12 years in building a vessel known as the "Western Ocean Yacht" aimed at the transatlantic trade, the characteristic features of this vessel are summarised as follows:

- Tonnage: two kinds of three masted topsail schooner were built; a *small* vessel of 93 to 99 ton, Plate 56, and an average tonnage of 97.2 ton; and a *larger* vessel of between 116 and 151 ton, and an average tonnage of 137 ton, Plate 57.
- Average dimensions of the *small* Porthmadog three mast topsail schooner have been calculated from data of the 11 vessels built; 91.66ft (28.1m) length x 22.76ft (6.98m) breadth x 10.59ft (3.25m) depth.

The L/B ratio = 4.02, and the B/D ratio = 2.14 indicate a narrow hull with relatively normal depth.

The *larger* three masted topsail schooner had the following average dimensions calculated from data of the 22 vessels built; 99.57ft (30.56m) length x 22.36ft (6.86m) breadth x 11.91ft (3.66m) depth.

The L/B ratio = 4.45 and B/D ratio = 1.87, indicate an increasingly narrow and deeper hull.

The larger schooner had its breadth reduced by 10% compared to the smaller schooner.

The three masted topsail schooners were long, narrow and relatively deep vessels carrying more cargo than the shorter and wider two masted schooners. A larger three masted topsail schooner had its breadth reduced by 20% compared to the 2 masted schooner. In total the vessels depth was roughly a half (46 to 53%) of the hull breadth in accordance with an Act of 1836.

- The hull shape, or form, is basically similar to that of the two masted schooner.

The *entrance,* or entry is a term used to describe the underwater hull body shape which contacts the water, and includes the cutwater which cuts the water before it reaches the vessels bow, or shoulders. Schooners have a short incurving entry. The stem is near vertical and sharp. See

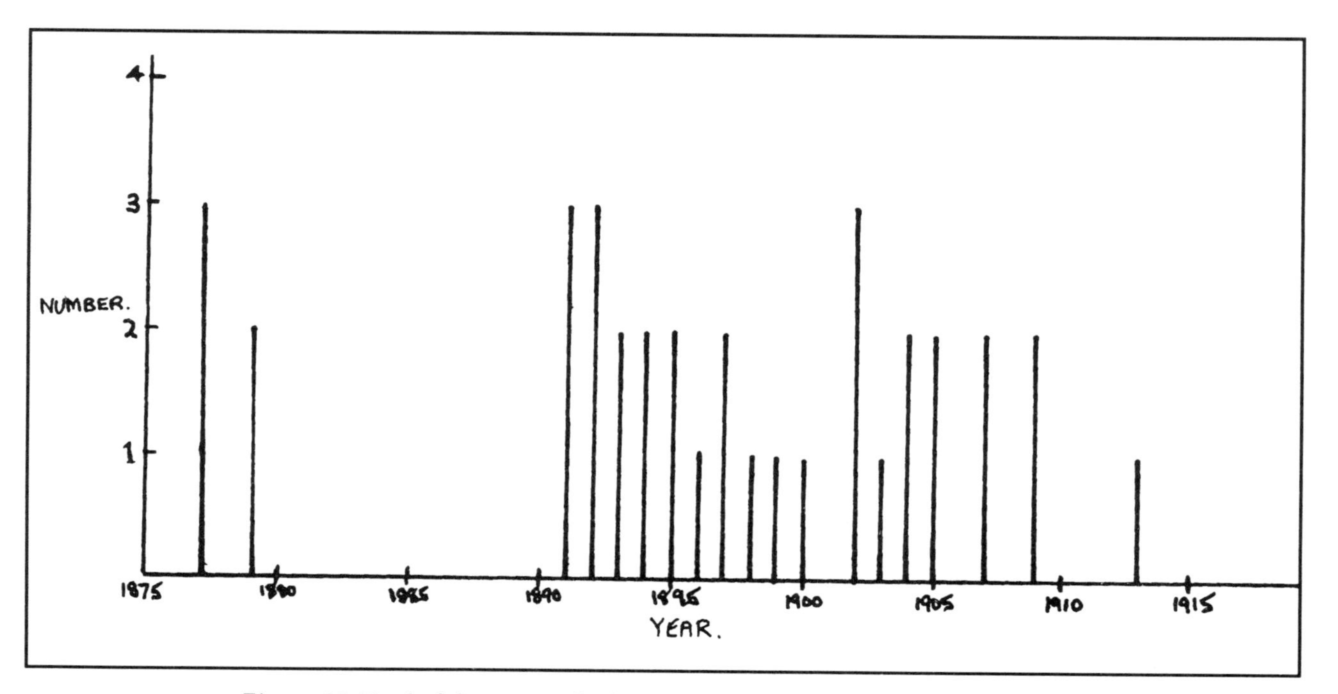

Figure 46. Total of three masted schooners built in Caernarfonshire 1875-1913.

Plates 56 and 57.

The *run* is a term for the underwater form of the after part of the vessel, which in a schooner is a long hollow run. See Plate 55. Caernarfonshire schooners have square sterns or transoms beneath which is the counter. See Plate 54.

Completing the hull form is the attractive *sheer line*, or curve of the hull upper edge running from stem to stern, and closely following the line of the upper sheer plank or gunwale – this is a notable and distinguishing feature of Porthmadog schooners, seen in Plate 54, 56 and 57.

All these three dimensional structural features of the hull: entry, run and sheer, are best appreciated when appraising a ship model hull, Plate 55, or the vessel in a dry dock, Plate 16.

• The three masts of the topsail schooner, Figure 47 (a), are named from the bow: foremast (1), mainmast (2) and mizzenmast (3).

Each mast is two part composed of lower mast and upper topmast joined together at the "crosstrees" masthead assembly. The bowsprit is a single spar and steeply steeved at an angle to the horizon.

The main mast is slightly taller than the other two masts. The masts of a three-mast topsail schooner are taller than two mast schooners.

• Sail rig of the three mast topsail schooner is shown in Figure 47 (a).

a) *headsails:* from the bowsprit end, flying jib (4), outerboom-jib (5), standing jib (6), fore-staysail (7).
b) *gaffsails:* gaff foresail (8), gaff mainsail (9) with main gaff topsail (10), gaff mizzensail (11) and mizzen gaff topsail (12) – both gaff topsails are jib-headed. See Figure 40.
c) *mast staysail:* main topmast staysail (13).
d) *square sails:* fore lower topsail (14), fore upper topsail (15), and the topgallant sail (16). The standing topgallant sail is the distinguishing feature of the Porthmadog three masted topsail schooner, which is also called a *double topsail topgallant yard* schooner.

As in all schooners a *running square sail* (17) was set to the foreyard for use in fair weather. In addition triangular shape

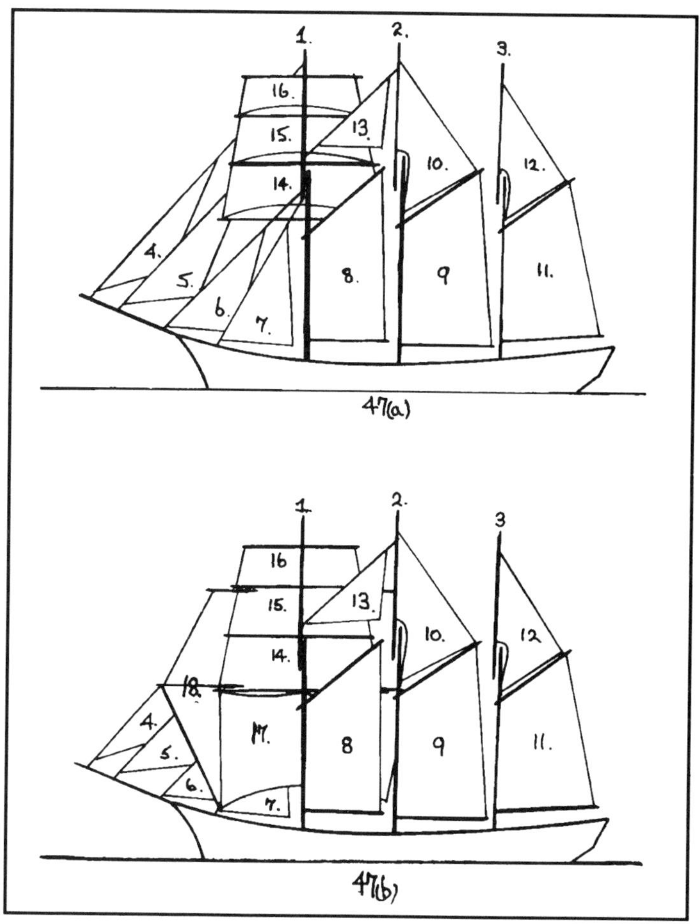

Figure 47. (a) Three masted schooner,double topsail, and topgallant rig; also (b) with studding sails and running square sail.

studding sails, or *stunsails* (18), were also set in three masted schooners during favourable weather when running before the wind. This was known as "putting on the muslin" as shown in Figure 47 (b), and frequently shown in schooner paintings. Plate 56.

Conversion of two masted schooners into three masted schooners often took place.

• Usage of the three masted topsail schooner was primarily for the transatlantic trade to Newfoundland for salt cod or dried stockfish, the Mediterranean, North Africa, for fresh fruits, and North Europe, Norway, Sweden, Denmark and the coastal trade to England.

Flying topgallant yards, were seen in the coastal trading schooners.

Standing topgallant fixed yards, were seen in the deepwater foreign-going schooners.

Cymru a'r Môr articles relating to schooners include:
"The schooner *Factor*, Barmouth 1836", Lewis Lloyd, Vol 2, 1977.
"The *Mary Mitchell*", Aled Eames, Vol 4, 1979.
"The schooner *Waft*", P.E.Herron,Vol 4, 1979.
"Life aboard a Cardiff trading schooner", P. E. Herton, Vol 5, 1980.
"Schooner *Unicorn*,Caernarfon"R.Turner, Vol 11,1987.
"Schooner *Eleanor and Jane*, Morfa Nefyn", I. W. Griffiths, Vol 12, 1989.
"History of topsail schooner *Mary Ashburner*", T. J. Latham, Vol 13, 1990.
"The three masted topsail schooner *Alert*", R. Hall, Vol 16, 1994.
"Memories of the Porthmadog schooner *M and A James*", B. Greenhill, Vol 17 1995.

13. SQUARE RIG VESSELS - One

The appendix 2 of *Hen Longau Sir Gaernarfon* records that over 190 square rigged vessels were built in Caernarfonshire, comprising 14% of the total vessels built during the period 1750 to 1910.

Square rig vessels are a class which includes; *brigantines, barquentines, brigs, barques and full rigged, (FR), ships,* all of which share the following common structural characteristics of the class:

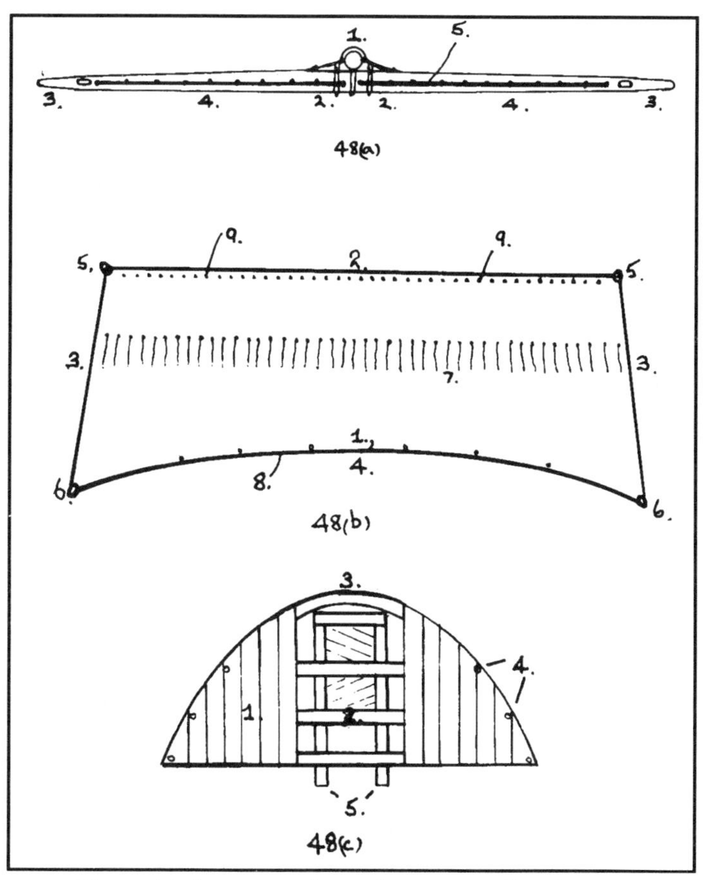

Figure 48. Structure of a yard, a squaresail and a top.

• Square, or foursided sails, are bent to horizontal yards arranged athwartship on the square rigged masts.

• The wooden square rigged mast is composed of three or four parts: lower mast, topsail mast, topgallant mast and royal mast. The fore-and-aft rigged masts when present are *two* part masts. Plate 32.

(Note: steel FR ships, barques, and modern square rigged vessels, could have *two* part masts: the lower and top masts were *combined* in one part without doublings, with separate parts topgallant and royal masts above.)

• The square rigged mast, has a full set of square sails, or is fully square rigged with: *course sail, topsails, topgallant sails, and royals,* see Plates 33, 60, 62, 63 and 71.

• At least ***one*** mast is fully square rigged in a square rig vessel.

• A *top* is present on the square rigged mast. See Plate 31.

It is not essential for a square riggged vessel to have fore-and-aft rigged masts – the following summary shows that *brigs* and *full rigged ships* are without.

VESSEL TYPE	TOTAL NUMBER OF MASTS	FULLY SQUARE RIGGED MASTS	FULLY FORE -AND-AFT RIGGED MASTS
Brigantine	Two	One	One
Brig	Two	All	None
Full Rigged Ship	Three or more (maximum five)	All	None
Barque	Three or more (maximum six)	All except the aftermost	One, the aftermost
Barquentine	Three or more (maximum six)	One, the foremast	All Except the foremast

Square rigged ships could only be commanded by a Master having the BOT (1850) competency certificate of Ordinary Master-able to command also steamships and fore-and-aft vessels.

Spars are wooden poles or rods used mainly to support the sails and include: masts, booms, gaffs, sprits, battens and yards.
Yards specifically support the square sails, lateen sails and lug sails.

Square Sail Yard
A square sail yard is shown in Figure 48 (a), it is suspended horizontally at right angles to the mast, and crossed or held to the mast by means of a parrel (parral) (1) a band of rope, or an iron collar, around the mast allowing the yard to slide up and down the mast. Instead of a parral, a shoe sliding in a track can be present.

The yard can also be *fixed* to the mast by means of a *truss band*. See Plate 25.

The middle of the yard is called the *slings* (2), and the yard tapers to its ends called the *yard arms* (3). Between the slings and yard arms are the *yard quarters* (4). Iron rods, or ropes, fixed longitudinally along the length of the yard are called *jackstays* (5).

The yards are named according to the mast part they connect with; *lowermast yard, topmast yards;* upper and lower topmast yards; and *topgallant yards;* upper and lower topgallant yards. A *royal yard* is above the topgallant yard.

The *crossjack,* crojack, yard is the lower mast yard of the mizzen mast-it is also the name of the lower mast yard, or foreyard, in fore-and-aft vessels which set a running square sail.

The Top
The *top,* shown in Figure 48 (c), is the name given to the, semi-circular shaped lower masthead assembly of a three, or four, part mast in all square rigged vessels, and is located below the "crosstrees" – see Figure 28. It is similar in construction to the topmast assembly "crosstrees", in addition it has *deck planking* (1) over the *crosstrees* (2), and a *rim* (3) at the edge connecting with the *futtock shrouds* (4). The whole structure is supported by the *trestletrees* (5) joined to the masthead *cheeks*. See Plate 31. The top functions to bind and support the mast parts together in the doubling, and to

extend and support the shrouds; it is also a platform for *topmen* working aloft.

Top Development

The top, in early square rigged vessels, such as: galleons, men-of-war and merchantmen, was of a square, shallow basket or saucer shape, see Plates 37 and 69. It was generally found as the lower masthead assembly of the fore, main and mizzen masts, and collectively called the "lower tops". It could also be found on the spritsail topmast. Similar tops could also be found at the topmast, and topgallant mast heads and were collectively called "upper tops". They are seen in pictures of naval training brigs for example the *Royalist*, see Plates 28, 29, 30 and 67.

In later vessels the "lower top" became a flat platform with a halfround or semicircular shape shown in Figure 48(c). After the 1750s the "upper tops" of square rigged vessels were reduced to "crosstrees", without decking and rims as shown in Figure 28.

Square Sails

Square sail structure is shown in the afterside view in, Figure 48 (b). The square sails are four sided or rectangular and composed of canvas *cloths* sewn together, the edges are strengthened by a boltrope (1), connected around the head (2), leeches (3) and foot (4). Cringles are found in each corner-head earing cringle (5), clew cringle (6). Reef points (7) are used to reduce the sail area. The square sail foot is curved in the *roach* (8) – this sail curvature serves to keep the sail clear of stays when the yards are moved during bracing. The roach is found also on gaff topsails.

The square sail is *bent* to the yard by connecting its head to the jackstays by means seizings of *rope bands* (robands) through the sail *eyelet holes* (9) and around the jackstay (5).

Square sails are named according to the yards they are bent to: *topmast* sails, *topgallant* sails and *royal* sails.

The *lower mast* yards connect with the fore-sail, main-sail, and mizzen-sail; also called the fore *course*, main *course*, and mizzen *course-crossjack* sails. See Plates 61, 62, 63, 66, 70, 71 and 72.

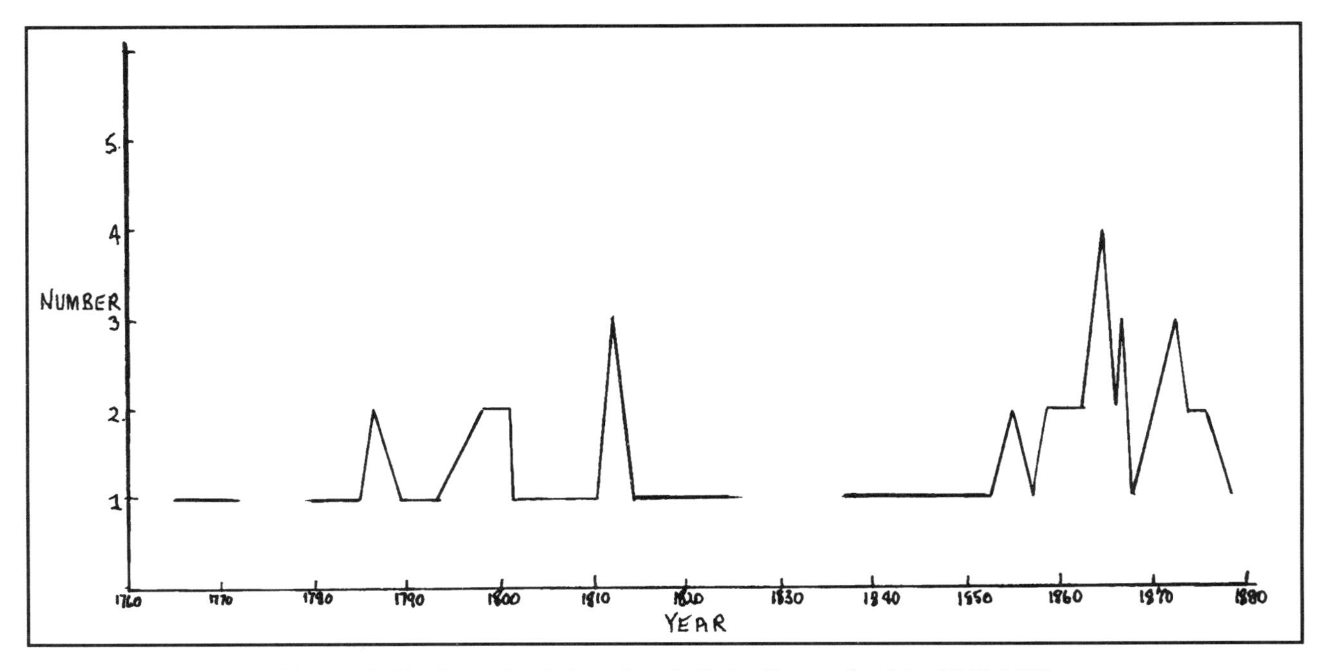

Figure 49. Total number brigantines built in Caernarfonshire 1760-1880.

Brigantines, Plates 58, 59 and 60.

Brigantines existed before 1700, the first brigantine recorded in *HLSG* is dated 1761 ahead of the first schooners recorded in 1795. For a time during the 1850s brigantines were called "schooners", to add to the confusion they were also called "hermaphrodite brigs", and "brig-schooners", the latter name arose from a vessel half brig and half fore-and-aft schooner.

The total number of brigantines recorded under that name in *HLSG* is 58, the peak periods are shown in the graph, Figure 49, between 1784 and 1878; the sloop building boom; also between 1840-1818, the schooner building boom. Most of the brigantines were built either in Pwllheli or Porthmadog.

The following summarises the characteristic features of brigantines:

• Tonnage: the tonnage of vessels built ranges from 65 to 230 ton, the graph Figure 50, shows the tonnage distribution with smaller brigantines ranging from 65 to 110 ton and

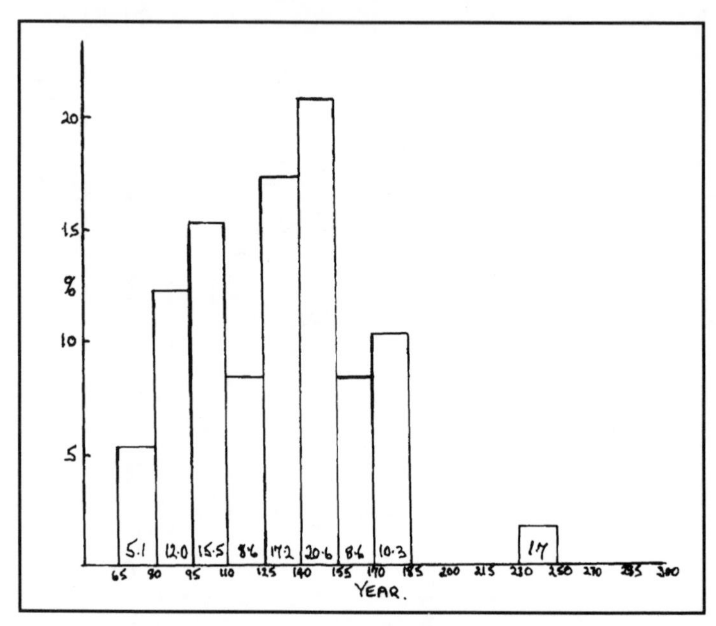

Figure 50. Tonnage of Caernarfonshire brigantines.

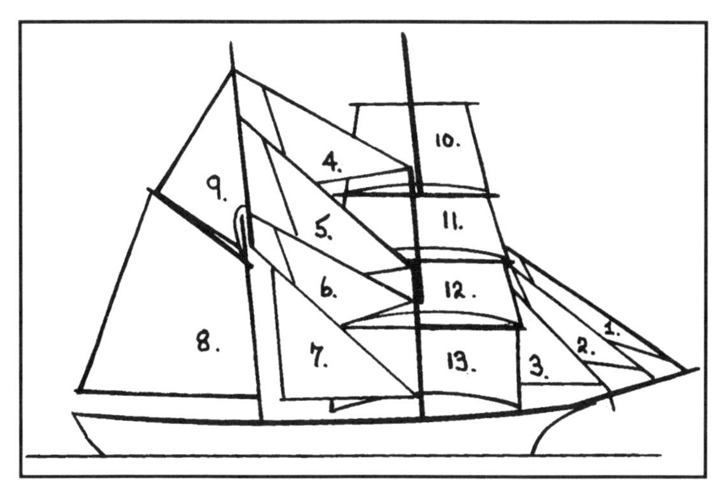

Figure 51. A brigantine rig.

larger brigantines ranging from 110 to 185 ton. The overall average was 147 ton.

• Dimensions; the following average dimension is obtained from a random selection of data: 92.76ft length x 22.4ft (6.9m) breadth x 11.7ft (28.5m) depth.

The L/B ratio = 4.14 and B/D ratio = 1.9, both these ratios indicate a narrow hull of relatively normal depth. A comparison of the average dimensions with a large three masted topsail schooner with those of the average brigantine is shown as follows:

Type	Tonnage	Length	Breadth	Depth	L/B	B/D
Three-mast schooner	137ton	91.6ft (28.1m)	22.7ft (6.96m)	10.59ft (3.25m)	4.0	2. 1
Brigantine	147ton	92.76ft (28.5m)	22.4ft (6.87m)	11.7ft (3.59m)	4.1	1.9

The similarity between the large three mast topsail schooner and brigantine is close, this relationship could indicate how the schooner developed from a brigantine. It also shows how a schooner could be easily converted into a brigantine.

• The hull structure of the brigantine also closely resembles that of the schooner previously described.

• Brigantines had only *two* masts named the foremast and mainmast.

The foremast was *three part* composed of lower mast, topmast and topgallant mast. The foremast had a top and "crosstrees" above.

The mainmast was *two part*, lower mast and topmast with "crosstrees" and no top. See Plates 58 and 59.

• The sail rig of a typical coasting brigantine is shown in Figure 51, the different sails are named as follows:

a) *headsails*: from bowsprit end; outer jib (1), inner jib (2), foretopmast staysail (3).
b) *mast staysails*: main topgallant staysail (4), maintopmast staysail (5), middle staysail (6), main staysail (7).
c) *gaff sails*: gaff sail (spanker, driver), (8), gaff topsail (9).
d) *square sails*: the foremast is fully square rigged; fore topgallant (10), fore upper topsail (11), fore lower topsail (12) and the fore course or foresail (13).

The usage of brigantines was mainly in coastal work, and to a lesser extent in European and Transatlantic trades. Contemporary brigantines have circumnavigated the world, for example the *Soren Larsen*, Plate 60 was a former visitor to Caernarfon and has sailed twice from UK to New Zealand where she now remains.

Barquentines, Plates 61, 62 and 63.

Eleven barquentines are recorded in *HLSG* as being built during 1857 to 1901, the main period of building was from 1862 to 1878 followed by a short period from 1884 to 1901. Most of this type of vessel was built in Porthmadog with the remainder at Pwllheli, Nefyn, and Borth-y-gest.

The following summarises the characteristic features of the barquentine;

• Tonnage ranged between 150 to 250 ton, the average being 228 ton. This large cargo capacity of a barquentine met the demands for big cargo carriers of the 1850s.

• Dimensions obtained from limited sources produced the following average dimensions: 110ft (33.8m) length x 25.01ft (7.67m) breadth x 13.9ft (4.26m) depth.

The L/B ratio = 4.39 and the B/D ratio = 1.80, indicating a narrow vessel with a deeper hull than the three masted schooners and brigantines.

• The hull of a barquentine is longer and slightly narrower than a large three masted topsail schooner and is deeper by about 15% indicating its greater cargo capacity, and also has the typical form of a schooner hull previously described.

• Local built barquentines had *three* masts, but upto six were possible in the larger vessels of over 500 tons built elsewhere.

• The three masts were named: foremast, mainmast and mizzen mast.

• The foremast was three part composed of lower mast, topmast and topgallant mast, together with a top and "crosstrees" above.

The main and mizzen masts were two part composed of lower mast and topmast, together with "crosstrees" and no top.

• The sail rig of a barquentine is fully square rigged on the foremast and fore-and-aft on the main and mizzen masts see Figure 52 (a), also Plates 61, 62 and 63. (The multimast barquentines may be fully square rigged on another mast.)

a) *headsails:* flying jib (1), outer boom jib (2), inner-standing jib (3), fore staysail (4).
b) *mast staysails:* main topgallant staysail (5), main topmast staysail (6), main staysail (7).
c) *gaff sails:* gaff main sail (8), main gaff topsail (9), gaff mizzen sail (10) and mizzen gaff topsail (11).
d) *square sails:* the foremast is fully square rigged on all mast parts; fore topgallant (12), fore upper topsail (13), fore lower topsail (14) fore course or fore sail (15). In addition a barquentine could carry upper topgallant sail, royal sails, and studding sails on the foremast, the latter were used in fair weather.

The vessels shown in the Figure 52 (a) and Plates 61, 62 and 63 are described as a *double topsail, single topgallant* barquentines.

Jack Barquentines

This vessel shown in Figure 52 (b), and Plate 64, was *intermediate* in its sail rig between the three masted

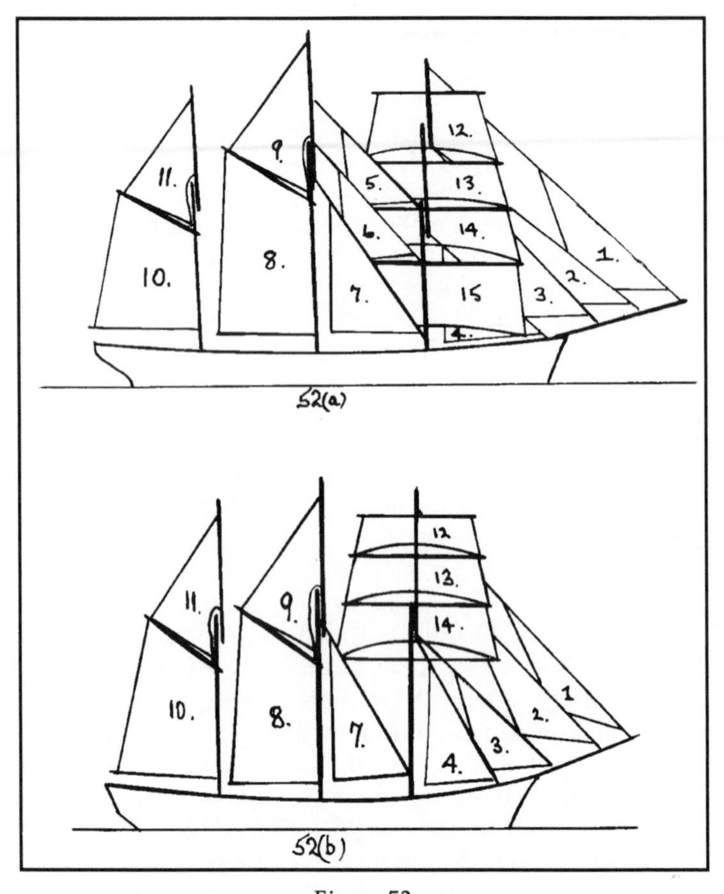

Figure 52.
(a)A barquentine, double topsail and single topgallant rig.
(b) A jack barquentine .

barquentine and the three masted schooner. It appeared following the decline of the barquentine and brig, and was intended to run more economically than the afore mentioned vessel types in the Newfoundland fish trade; it also could be commanded by a master with only a fore-and-aft masters certificate of competency.

The vessel partly resembled the three mast schooner, see Figure 47a, in the following characteristics:

(a) all three masts were *two part*. No mast was three part as in a barquentine. No top was present on the foremast.
(b) the square sails included; two topsails and a topgallant, with running square sail on fore yard.
(c) the gaff sails were present on the main and mizzen masts only. Unlike the three masted schooner, Figure 47, the gaff sail was absent from the foremast, instead there were upto three *mainmast staysails.*

The Jack Barquentine was not in any way a square rigged vessel because of the *absence* of a top and three part masts.

The sail rig of the jack barquentine shown in Figure 52 (b) is labelled in the same way as the barquentine.

Five jack barquentines were built in Porthmadog between 1873 and 1876, they were regarded as the fore-runners of the three masted schooner which appeared from 1891 onwards. The jack barquentine was easy to convert to the traditional three masted schooner. See Plate 65.

14. SQUARE RIGGED VESSELS - Two

The commonest types of merchant sailing vessel to be seen during the 1700s was the two masted square rigged vessel called the *brig* together with the closely similar square rigged vessel called the *snow*; the former mainly engaged in short coastal voyages, and the latter in longer ocean voyages.

Brigs, Plates 66, 67 and 68.
Merchant and naval brigs existed from the 1600s and flourished until about 1870 when they were replaced by the larger barques and full rigged ships. *Hen Longau Sir Gaernarfon* Appendix 2 records that 71 brigs were built in Caernarfonshire during the years 1750 to 1900, see Figure 53. Most of the brigs were built in Porthmadog, followed by Pwllheli, Nefyn and Conwy. The peak building period was in 1860 to 1875 prior to their extinction after a very long

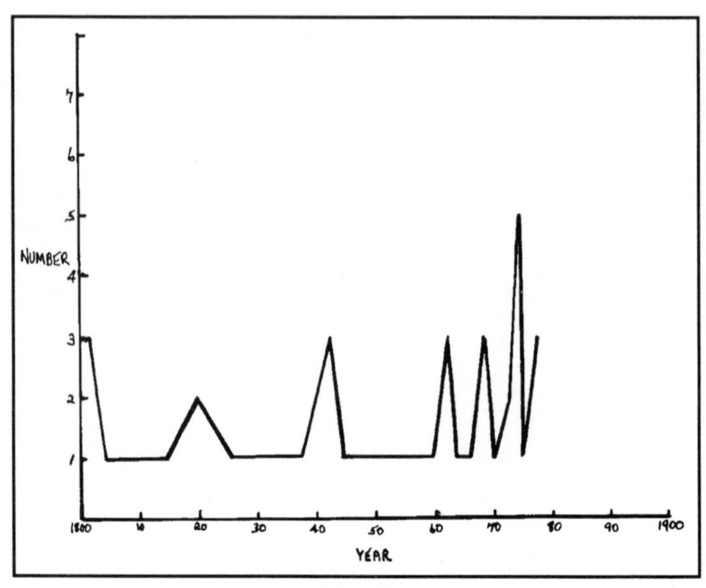

Figure 53.
Total number of brigs built in Caernarfonshire 1800-1880.

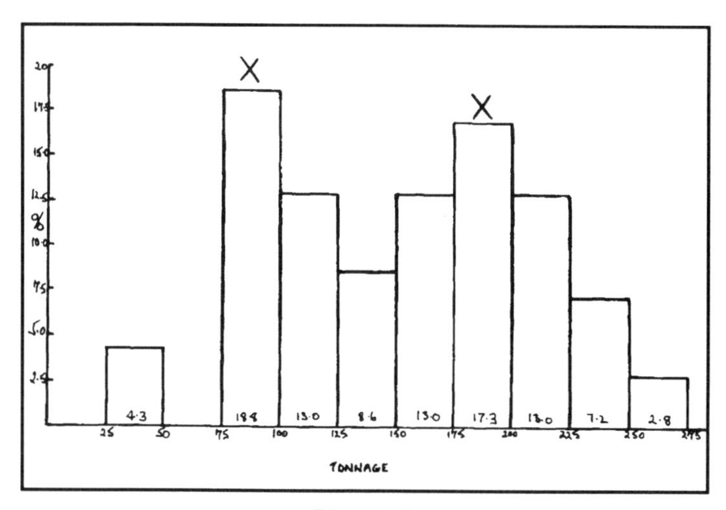

Figure 54.
Tonnage of Caernarfonshire brigs.

period of existence of over 200 years. The following summarises the main characteristics of these two masted vessels, fully square rigged on all masts:

• Tonnage ranged from 25 to 275 ton as shown in the tonnage distribution graph Figure 54. The graph indicates that two main varieties of brigs were built; the *smaller* brig comprising 35% of the total built with a tonnage range between 25 and 125 ton – overall average 125 ton; and the *larger* brig comprising 65% of the total built with a tonnage range between 125 and 275 ton, or an average 201 ton.

• Dimensions of the small brigs averaged; 67.4ft (20.7m) length x 21.1ft breadth (6.5m) x 11.6ft (3.56m) depth.

The L/B ratio = 3.19 indicated a relatively beamy hull, and the B/D ratio = 1.81 indicated a deep hull.

The large brigs averaged: 105ft (32.2m) length x 24.5ft (7.5m) breadth x 13.3 ft (4.1m) depth.

The L/B ratio = 4.28, indicating a much narrower hull than the small brig.

The B/D ratio = 1.84, indicating a deep hull similar to the small brig – both types having a high cargo capacity.

• The wooden hull form was boxlike, and very strongly

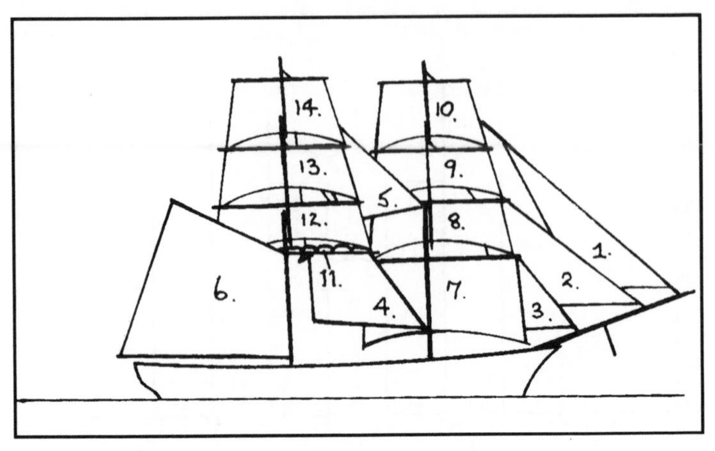

Figure 55.
A brig, double topsail and single topgallant rig.

built without attractive lines – but ideal for heavy cargo carriage. The stem was straight and the bows bluff, the stern was square with a transom and counter beneath. Small brigs often had to take the ground and their flat bottoms had comparitively little deadrise and the vessel remained upright.

• Brig masting consisted of two masts, named foremast and main mast of equal height and were composed of three parts; lower mast, topmast and topgallant mast. Each mast had a top with "crosstrees" above. The naval training brigs had two tops to each mast; a "lower" and "upper" top as seen in the Plates 28, 29 and 30.

The sail rig is shown in Figure 55 and the sails named as follow:

a) *headsails:* normally two headsails but three could be set; from the jibboom end they are named as: flying jib (1), jib (2) and the foretopmast staysail (3).
b) *mast staysails:* main topmast staysail (4), main topgallant staysail (5).
c) *gaff sail:* the gaff main sail (6) is also called a spanker or driver. This sail has a hoisting gaff spar and a boom and its luff is connected by hoops to the lower main mast.

d) *Square sails*: **after 1850**, each mast was fully square rigged as follows.

The *foremast*: foresail, or fore course (7), fore lower topsail (8) and fore upper topsail (9) fore top gallant sail (10). No royals were set.

The *main mast*: main sail or main course (11) shown furled in the Figure; main lower topsail (12), main upper topsail (13) and main topgallant sail (14). Royal sails were seldom set.

This type of brig rig was known as a *double topsail, single topgallant* brig. See Plate 66.

The **pre-1850** brigs were called single topsail, single topgallant brigs; their topsails were later divided after 1850 into lower and upper topsails as described above.

The early brigs were often without a mainsail, or main course, see Plate 67 and 68, and those after 1850 had the mainsail, or main course, furled (11) as in Figure 55, this is frequently seen in pictures of old brigs – the purpose of the furled sail was to prevent obstruction to the large main topmast staysail ahead.

• The Caernarfonshire built brigs were used mainly in coastal work, with the remainder in voyages to Europe, and foreign going to Newfoundland, West Indies and South Africa.

• The brig *Mary Winch*, 252 ton, built 1884 at Pwllheli was one of the towns notable vessels that was sold in 1853 to the Black Ball Line of Liverpool, a shipping company with a fleet of fast clipper ships.

• Some vessels called *revenue* brigs were built on cutter hulls and rigged as fully squared rigged brigs, they are to be seen in old paintings and pictures and show an ornate carved stern with an ensign at the stern ensign staff.

Snows

The snow was a two masted sailing vessel, fully square rigged on each mast, as shown in Figure 56, and was in existence for many years from the 1600s until the early 1800s. Seven vessels were built in Pwllheli between 1800 and 1835.

• Their tonnage ranged between 75 and 250 ton, the average tonnage of a snow being 123 ton.

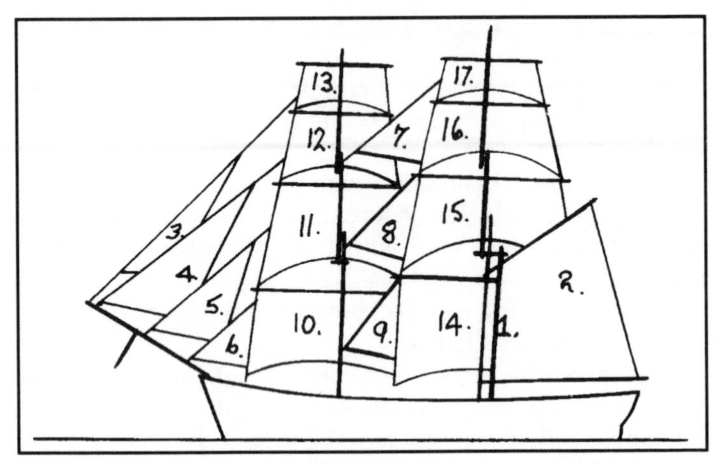

Figure 56.
A snow, single topsail, and single topgallant ,with royals rig.

• The dimensions averaged as follows: 85.5ft (26.25m) length x 22.4ft (6.88m) breadth x 13.26ft (4.1m) depth.

The L/B ratio = 3.8 indicated a narrow hull. The B/D ratio = 1.68 indicated a *deeper* cargo carrying hull than for a brig. Otherwise the beam was intermediate between large and small brigs

• The general hull structure was closely similar to the brig.

• The main difference between the two types of vessel were to be found in the sail rig of lower main mast. The sail rig of a snow and brig are otherwise similar as shown in Figures 55 and 56.

• A *snow mast* or *trysail mast* (1) is the distinguishing feature of a snow and is found abaft of the main lower mast- this structure is fixed into the deck and into the topmast assembly. The luff of the gaff sail (2) or trysail – also called spanker or driver – is laced to this *trysail mast*, whereas in the brig there is no trysail mast and the gaff sail, or spanker, luff is connected to the *mainmast* by means of hoops.

The snow gaff sail (trysail spanker or driver) is usually smaller than the gaff sail of a brig, for the reason that a snow *sets* its main sail or main course, (14) whereas the brig keeps its furled or is without this sail.

• The snow complete rig in Figure 56, is described as being *single topsail, single topgallant with royals – the royal sails* were set more often in snows giving the vessel a greater sail area than brigs, as they were engaged in voyages of longer duration.

(a) *headsails:* flying jib (3), outer jib (4), jib (5), and fore topmast staysail (6).

(b) *mast staysails:* main royal staysail (7) main top gallant stay sail (8) and the main topmast staysail (9).

(c) *gaff sails:* gaff main sail (spanker, driver, or trysail) (2).

(d) *square sails*:

Fore mast: foresail or fore course (10), fore topsail (11), fore topgallant sail (12), fore royal sail (13).

Main mast: mainsail or main course (14), main topsail (15), topgallant sail (16), main royal sail (17).

Barques, Plates 69, 70 and 71

During the 1600s merchant and naval vessels included a range of types: sloops, cutters, ketches, brigantines, brigs and snows and many more quaintly named vessels. Amongst these names was the *bark* applied to a vessel with three or more masts, fully square rigged on all masts, except the aftermost, or mizzen, mast which was *fore-and-aft* rigged. The name bark continued in use until about 1850 when it became known as the *barque.*

The tradition of building barques in Caernarfonshire continued until 1877, before that time 21 barques had been recorded in *Hen Longau Sir Gaernarfon* as having been built since 1841; eight were built in Pwllheli, five in Porthmadog, three in Y Felinheli, two in Nefyn and one each in Caernarfon, Porth Dinllaen, and Conwy.

The brig lost its popularity by 1850 and was replaced from 1841 by the barque during the boom building period of wooden sailing vessels which ended in the 1870s, see Figure 42. The characteristics features of the barque type of sailing vessel are summarised as follows:

• Tonnage: the tonnage range extended from 210 to 825 ton, and an average of 362 ton. Some 57% of the barques were in the range 300 to 399 ton, and 24% in the range 200-

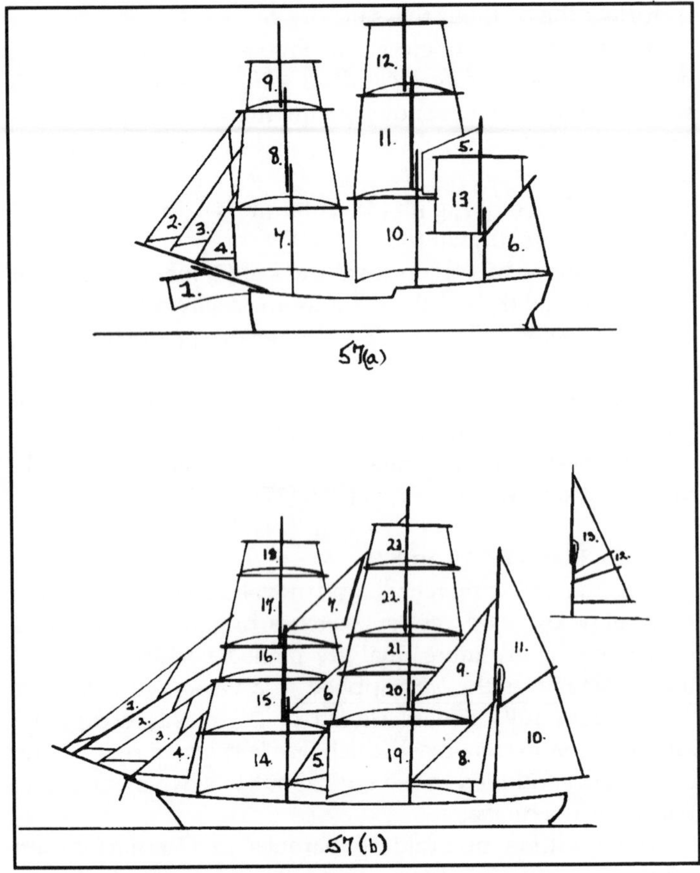

Figure 57. Barques, pre and post 1850.

299 ton. These tonnages indicated relatively small vessels.

• Dimensions: the average dimensions – 120ft (36.84m) length x 27.5ft (8.45m) breadth x 14.5ft (4.45m) depth.

The L/B ratio = 4. 36 and the B/D ratio = 1.89, indicate a long narrow and deep vessel similar to the large brig and barquentine.

• The hull of the early barques had straight stems and bluff bows; see Plate 69, showing the bows of the bark replica *Endeavour* with it deep hull rounded in section with a flat bottom. The stern was square with a transom. In general following the boxlike form of cargo carriers.

• Masting – the foremast and mainmast were composed of three parts: lower mast, topmast and topgallant mast, each mast had a top and "crosstrees" above.

The mizzen mast was composed of two of parts lower mast and upper mast with "crosstrees" only and no top.

A quarter deck was present.

The pre1850 barque sail rig. Figure 57(a)

The average small barque, Figure 57(a) built in Caernarfonshire during the 1750s were vessels resembling Captain James Cooks bark the 366 ton *Endeavour*, which had the dimensions 106ft (32.54m) length x 29ft (8.9m) breadth.

The following sail rig shown in Figure 57 (a) is typical of these early vessels.

a) *headsails*: below the bowsprit was the bowsprit sail, or spritsail (1). The sails from the end of the bows were; flying jib (2), outer jib (3), and jib or standing jib (4).
b) *mast staysails:* the only known sail set was the mizzen topmast stay sail (5) which was a *foursided* sail.
c) *gaff sail:* the original lateen sail had been cut down and a gaff mizzen sail (6) bent to a gaff spar replaced it. The gaff mizzen sail was loose footed without a boom.
d) *square sails*:

The *foremast* sails consisted of: foresail or fore course (7), fore topsail (8) and fore topgallant sail (9).

The *mainmast* sails were: mainsail or main course (10), main topsail (11) and main topgallant sail (12).

The *mizzen mast* had a mizzen topsail only (13).

The early barques were said to have a *single topsail, single topgallant* rig.

The 1850 to 1870 barque sail rig. Figure 57 (b)

The sail rig was composed as follows:

a) *headsails:* flying jib (1), outer jib (2), inner jib (3), and fore topmast staysail (4).
b) *mast staysails:* main staysail (5), main topmast staysail (6), and main topgallant staysail (7). Connected to the mizzen mast were, the mizzen staysail (8) and mizzen topmast staysail (9).
c) *gaff sails:* gaff sail, spanker or driver (10), this could

have a boom or could be loose footed, with gaff topsail (11). The mizzen mast in some barques could have upper gaff topsail (13) and lower gaff topsail (12) as shown in the small sketch inset Figure 57 (b). Many barques set a three sided trysail on the mizzen mast without a gaff.

d) *square sails*:

Foremast: fore course (14), fore lower topsail (15), fore upper topsail (16), fore topgallant sail (17) and fore royal sail (18).

Main mast: main course (19), main lower topsail (20), main upper topsail (21), main topgallant sail (22), and main royal sail (23).

This barque rig was described as being *double topsail, single topgallant, with royals*. See Plate 70.

The post 1890 barque sail rig, Figure 63 and Plate 71.

This rig was seen in the cargo carrying sailing barques during the declining years of sail, and was described as *double topsail, with double topgallant sails only*, with no sails above the topgallant sails. See the chapter "Full Rigged Sailing Ship".

Notable Barques

The sterling sailing qualities of Captain James Cooks bark *Endeavour* as a deepwater vessel, sailing worldwide, was emulated in the Caernarfonshire built barques, most of which were sold out of the county particularly to Liverpool. *Ordovic*, built 1875 at Y Felinheli, at 853 ton was the largest barque built in Caernarfonshire. Measuring 168.8ft (51.8m) length x 33.8ft (10.37m) breadth x 21.3 ft (6.54m) depth.

The L/B ratio = 4.99, and B/D ratio = 1.58, indicating a narrow and considerably deeper vessel than normal the *Ordovic* was wrecked of Cape Horn 1894.

Mary Holland, built as a brig in 1843 at Porthmadog, 233 ton and was converted to a barque in 1854 and purchased by James Baines owner of the clipper ship Black Ball line of Liverpool.

Henry Winch built 1845 at Pwllheli, 473 ton, also joined the Black Ball Line of Liverpool.

Charles Brownell, built 1846 at Pwllheli, 421 ton, sold to

Carter and Baines forerunners of the Black Ball Line.

The Black Ball line owned over 100 vessels engaged in carrying emigrants to North America and Australia, and troops to the Crimea. Amongst the fast clipper ships owned were the *Lightning, Red Jacket* and *James Baines*. Fast sailing passenger and cargo ships were needed on various trading routes and the new hull designs were sharp, rakish, and low in the water "clipper ships" – see the chapter on "Full Rigged Ship".

Loss of Barque Chief Officer from Trefor
Plate 74

Robert Hugh Jones, Plate 74, of Croeshigol House, Trefor, attended the local village school, and distinguished himself as being amongst the school's top scholars, and spent much of his early life, like most other Caernarfonshire youngsters, on the beach and aboard the fishing boats. Later he crewed on local schooners and rose from seaman to being a schoonerman holding a Masters certificate fore-and-aft.

The authors maternal grandmother told him how she made a voyage to Belfast aboard the schooner commanded by Captain Robert Hugh Jones, who was two years her senior. Evidently the young couple had a close relationship and also had parental approval for her to sail with the young schooner captain.

Deepwater sail called this young ambitious man who made voyages to Australia in the barque *Antofagasta*, and later, at the age of 24, and proudly holding a Masters square rig certificate of competency, joined the Whitehaven registered steel barque *Friars Crag* as Chief Officer, for her maiden voyage in 1892. No doubt he cherished ambitions of putting in seatime in order to make the change into steamships, which during the 1890s were rapidly displacing sail.

Taking on the responsible position as a very young First Officer, was a daunting task in a large vessel of 1433 ton – almost four times larger than the average Caernarfonshire barque with dimensions of 237.5ft (72.9m) length x 36.2ft (11.12m) breadth x 21.7ft (6.66m) depth. The L/B ratio = 6.5 and B/D ratio 1.66; indicating a very narrow and deep vessel with a high cargo capacity.

The barque sailed out of the Mersey eventually reaching Newcastle, New South Wales and after discharging cargo, sailed 22nd September 1892 for Iquique, Chile, South America, were she was to load nitrates. Disaster struck the barque in what can be some of the roughest seas between the east coast of Australia and the North Cape of New Zealand, where the vessel was lost with all hands.

A vessel's name board together with other wreckage came ashore at Woodsbluff, Clarence River, near Sydney - written on the name board in gilt letters was *Friars Crag.*

(Extracted from the *Sydney Morning Herald* – February 13th 1893 – a report by Pilot McCauley at Clarence River.)

Crew list:

Master: Gilpin Waddel of Whitehaven.

Chief Officer: Robert Hugh Jones, "Croeshigol House", Trefor, Caernarfonshire.

Second Officer: Samuel Duncan, Rothesay.

Apprentices: Charles James Watt, and William Herbert Watt, Birkenhead. Richard. J. Payne Portsmouth. William Mackereth and Thomas Tyson Kitchin of Whitehaven.

Boatswain: John Joseph Benson of Whitehaven.

Carpenter: John McPharson.

Cook: Robert Hutchinson.

Steward: W. Hall of South Shields.

Able seamen: John. A. Lynn and Lachlin Campbell of Glasgow.

John Buchanan of New York. John. J. Laird of Dundee.

John Taylor of Cork. Daniel Bodels of Magheramorne, Co Antrim.

John Walker, Thomas Devine, and James Clark of Whitehaven.

A. Cassie and F. Gardner of Newcastle NSW.

The *Friars Crag*, was a well found newly built vessel, and with a crew of 23 was well manned, and all the seamen were experienced able seamen. No third officer is listed and it is possible that a senior apprentice was the unqualified third officer, a common occurrence.

The tragic news of the loss of the *Friars Cràg* and all her crew, was eventually relayed to the Trefor Post Office where it was received by the local postmaster, the father of Captain Robert Hugh Jones. The sorrow and grief of Roberts parents were shared by my grandmother and the people of Trefor. His memorial is inscribed on his parents gravestone at Llanaelhaearn.

Cymru a'r Môr articles related to brigs, and barques include:
"Hanes y barque *Wandering Sprite*", Bedwyr Lewis, Vol 2, 1977.
"The *Fleetwing* of Porthmadog", Aled Eames, and M. K. Stammers. Vol 4, 1979.
"The Severn, Welsh brig lost in the Atlantic", D. Parham, Vol 20, 1999.

15. FULLY SQUARE RIGGED SAILING SHIP

The name for a fully square rigged sailing ship is shortened to full rigged (FR) ship, sailing ship, or just plain *ship* as in the registers.

The three masted, fully-rigged sailing ship had existed in its simplest form since the time of the English type galleons, man-of-war, and ship-of-the line, and later underwent development into the full rigged sailing ship built in Caernarfonshire and elsewhere during the 1800s.

Eight FR sailing ships were built in Caernarfonshire, six at Pwllheli and two at Conwy. The first four being built during 1790 to 1802, the boom building period for sloops, see Figure 15, and the next four during the period 1845 to 1848 a boom building period for two masted schooners, see Figure 42.

The FR sailing ship was a vessel distinct from the barque and possesed the following characteristics:

• Tonnage: the early Caernarfonshire FR sailing ships were of a small tonnage between 232 to 281 ton, during the later 1840s FR sailing ships were larger at 458 ton and not many were over 500 ton. Elsewhere in Britain during 1800 to 1880 the tonnage ranged between 300 to 1250 tons.

• The dimensions of the average 346 ton FR sailing ship for the period 1840 to 1860 was: 123ft (37.8m) length x 25.5ft (7.82m) breadth x 15.6ft (4.8m) depth.

The L/B ratio = 4.82 and B/D ratio = 1.63, indicating a narrow and deep hull.

Tracing the Development of the Caernarfonshire Sailing Vessel Hull 1750-1910

Given the FR sailing ships average dimensions in the following table, it is interesting to trace the change in hull dimensions which took place during the150 years from the early sloop, through the other types of wooden sailing vessel, to the culmination of the building of the FR sailing ship in Caernarfonshire.

Table: CAERNARFONSHIRE AVERAGE VESSEL DIMENSIONS – 1750-1910

Vessel	Length ft	m	Tonnage ton nett	L/B	B/D
Sloop	36.5	(10.3)	28.5	2.8	2.0
Smack	39.7	(12.2)	37.9	2.99	2.14
Cutter	69.0	(21.2)	-	3.0	2.3
Ketch	70.0	(21.5)	73.0	3.4	2.2
Two mast schooner	76.0	(23.3)	73.0	3.7*	1.9*
Small 3m schooner	91.0 *	(27.9)	96.0	4.02	2.14
Large 3m schooner	101.0	(31.0)	133.0 *	4.45	1.87
Brigantine	92.7	(28.4)	125.0	4.1	1.9
Barquentine	110.0	(33.8)	228.0	4.39	1.8
Small brig	67.0	(20.6)	125.0	3.19	1.81
Large brig	100.0	(30.7)	201.0	4.28	1.84
Barque	120.0	(36.8)	320.0	4.36	1.89
Small FR ship	123.0	(37.8)	347.0	4.82	1.63
AVERAGE VESSEL HULL DIMENSIONS =	84.3ft	(25.88m)	148.0ton	L/B=3.8	B/D=1.94

• It is evident from the table that the *average type* of Caernarfonshire vessel* was of the *schooner class;* having the average length of a small three masted schooner, and the average tonnage of a large three masted schooner, combined with the L/B and B/D ratios of a two mast schooner – indicating a narrow and deep hull, with average dimensions of: 84.3ft (25.88m) length x 22.18ft (6.80m) breadth x 11.4ft (3.5m) depth.

The popularity of the schooner class in Caernarfonshire is also confirmed by the total number of schooners built as being over 481 or 35% of the total of all kinds of vessels built.

• During the development of the Caernarfonshire wooden sailing vessel over a period of 150 years from 1750 to 1900, the evolving hull had generally become *long* and *narrow* with with a relatively constant depth as indicated by the B/D and L/B ratios.

• The average L/B ratio of a sloop = 2.8, this was 40% beamier than a FR sailing ship; similarly the three masted schooner average L/B ratio = 4.02, was 20% beamier than the FR sailing ship, confirming the view that as the hull developed it became *narrower* over a period of time.

• The average length of the evolving hull increased from 36.5ft (11.2m) in sloops, to 76ft (23.3m) in two masted schooners, to 123ft (37.76m) in FR sailing ships.

• The average tonnage increased from 28.5 ton for sloops, to 96 ton for small three masted schooners, to 346 ton for FR sailing ships.

Pre 1850 Full Rigged Sailing Ship

• Prior to 1850 the FR sailing ship was a comparitively slow vessel with average speeds of around 5 knots and having the following basic structural features:

a) heavily built boxlike hull.
b) straight stem and stern (Figures 25 and 61).
c) bluff bows.
d) short, beamy, flat bottomed hull.
e) high freeboard and deep draught.

• Masting – the number of masts in a Caernarfonshire FR sailing ship was usually three, named: fore, main and mizzen masts.

Much larger vessels were to be built elsewhere with upto five masts.

• The masts were three part; lowermast, topmast and topgallant mast, each with a lower top and upper, masthead assembly. The upper masthead assembly being called the "crosstrees".

• All square rigged vessels built before 1850 namely: brigs, brigantines, barquentines, barques and FR sailing ships, were rigged with the same set of square sails, collectively composed of: *courses, single topsails, single topgallants,* with *royal* square sails; see Figure 58. This arrangement is seen also in earlier square rigged vessels, merchantman and man-of-war, see Figures 13 and 14.

• The presence of *single* topsails and *single* topgallants identified the FR ships period as being pre 1850.

• The sail rig components in Figure 58 are named as

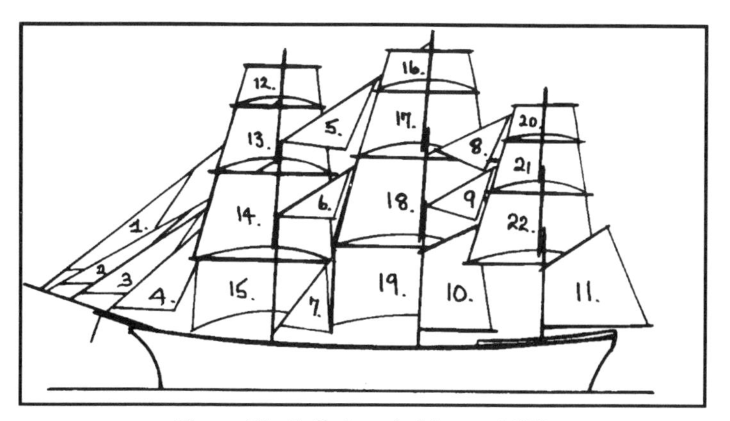

Figure 58. Full rigged ship, pre1850.

follows:

a) *headsails:* flying jib (1), outer jib (2), inner jib (3), foretopmast staysail (4). The jib boom appears after 1720 and replaces the spritsail topmast seen in earlier vessels.

b) *mast staysails:* main royal staysail (5), main topgallant staysail (6), main topmast staysail (7). Mizzen royal staysail (8), mizzen topgallant staysail (9).

c) *gaff sails:* some FR ships had sails called *spencers* on the fore and main masts that were laced to the standing gaff. Only the main spencer (10) is shown in the Figure 58. Spencers could be without a boom or loose-footed.

The gaff sail (11) also called the spanker or driver, could also have a gaff topsail not shown in the diagram. (See Figure 57b.)

d) *square sails:* the sail rig in Figure 58 is described as ***single*** *topsails,* ***single*** *topgallants,* with royals.

Fore mast sails: fore royal sail (12), fore topgallant sail (13), fore topsail (14), and fore course (15).

Main mast sails: main royal sail (16), main topgallant sail (17), main topsail (18), and main course (19).

Mizzen mast sails: mizzen royal sail (20), mizzen topgallant sail (21) and mizzen topsail (22). The mizzen crojack sail or mizzen course sail was not often bent to the

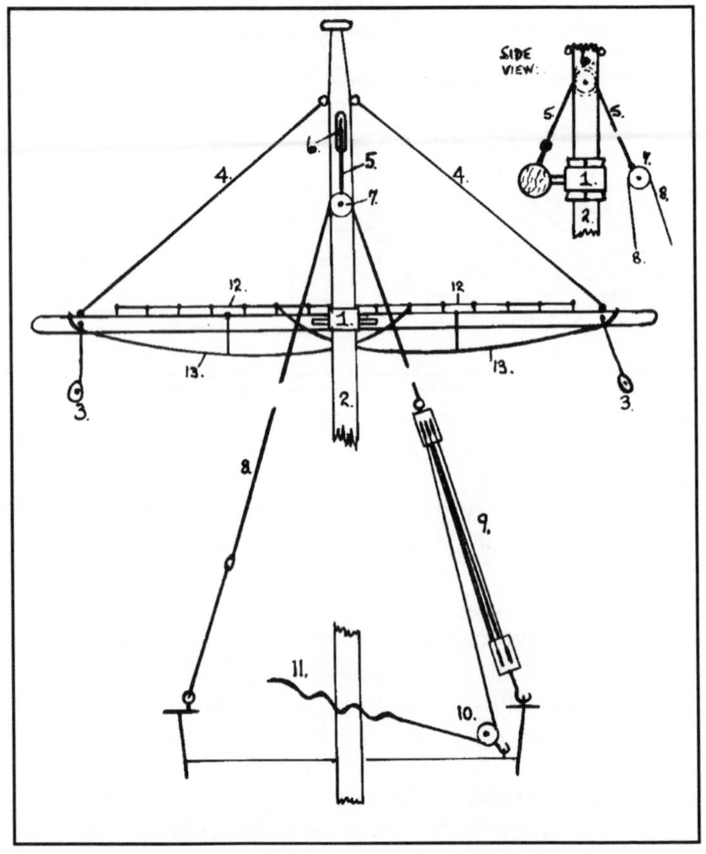

Figure 59. Hoisting yard,running rigging.

yard, the absence of this sail allowed the main spencer (10) to operate effectively.

Running Rigging

Yards, square sails and fore-aft-sails form the propulsion unit of a sailing vessel which is operated or controlled by the *running rigging gear,* namely *purchases* and *tackles*, which are composed of lines, ropes, wire or chain roved through *blocks* (pulleys). The blocks are simple machines which allow large loads to be moved by means of a small effort of *man-power* in "pulley hauley".

VESSEL TYPES

Plate 36. ***Clinker built boat****; a traditionally built clinker rowing boat built at Classic Sailingboats, Bethel, displays all the characteristics of the Scandinavian clinker vessels, the only concession to modernity is the transom stern. The hull is built as a shell and planked around a mould, when completely planked up the ribs are inserted, followed by stringers and thwarts. (Classic Sailboats, Bethel)*

Plate 37. ***Ketch;*** *this replica the 'Nonsuch' depicts a vessel known as a 'bomb ketch' of the 1600s, and was used in the transatlantic crossing of the Hudson Bay Company and the establishment of the fur trading company in Canada in 1670. The vessel appears to have the strongly built hull of a small three-masted carrack from which the foremast has been removed. It also has the features of a small galleon in the presence of two part masts, square topsails, staysail, and wreaths around the gunports. Removal of the foremast provides a large forward deck area ideal for a cargo carrier or a mortar cannon – hence the name 'bomb ketch'. The sail rig identifies the vessel as a ketch.*

Plate 38. ***Sloop at Porthsgadan****; The vessel has a deep carvel built hull, straight stem and square transom stern. Smoke is emerging from the focsle bogey stove pipe. The deck has the typical low bulwark of a sloop. The gaff spar is near the masthead and the gaff sail is furled on the boom. The long bowsprit is standing or fixed and the headsails are furled. (G. Jones)*

Plate 39. ***Sloop at Felinheli****; A typical small sloop cargo carrier, taking the ground upright due to the lack of deadrise in the hull. In the background is another coastal trader in the form of a single topsail schooner. (Gwynedd Archives)*

Plate 40. ***Sloop at Aberdovey 1834****; The vessel in the foreground has a straight stem and bluff bows together with a square stern. The hull is carvel planked with little deadrise to take the ground upright, and the bulwarks are low. The two part mast has a topmast which has been lowered below the "crosstrees". The bowsprit is standing and the standing jib on hanks is furled. The gaff sail is lowered. Immediately in the background another sloop shows its topmast above the "crosstrees", and its gaff spar is at the masthead. To the left background there is a two masted single topsail schooner. (National Library Of Wales)*

Plate 41. ***Smack****; a smack having set her fine weather sails; running square sail and single topsail, off the Llŷn coast. From a painting.*

Plate 42. ***North Wales nobby;*** *A small fishing cutter of the nobby type seen at Pwllheli. The hull has a rounded stem with a rounded counter stern and a low freeboard. A low rail or outer coaming is present, together with a coaming surrounding the open cockpit which contain the fishing gear. The single pole mast is rigged with a gaff sail and a single jib connects with bowsprit end. Steering is by means of a tiller. (Gwynedd Archives)*

Plate 43. ***Model nobby;*** *the model shows the fine lines of the hull and curved stem with a fine entrance to the bow, the bowsprit heel is fixed betwen two bitts, and a small fife rail with its belaying pins is afore the mast foot. A samson post and nogs together with a focsle hatch and bogey stove pipe are located on the foredeck. The characteristic main thwart or thoft is within the cockpit and a bilge pump is located on the portside deck midships.*
(Author, and "cimwch. com")

Plate 44. ***Lancashire nobby****; This Lancashire nobby was originally built at Ulverston 1912 and was used for trawling in Morecambe Bay. After a working life of over ninety years the vessel underwent extensive reconstruction during 2005-06, as shown in Plates 8 to 13 at Waterfront Marine boatyard, Porth Penrhyn. In this splendid picture Scott Metcalfe, the boatyard proprietor, skippers the nobby under her gaff sail, and two jibs, following her relaunching in 2007. (Mike Arridge, Pentir)*

Plate 45. ***Trearddur bay dinghy****; this smart sailing dinghy with its dipping lug-sail is produced to a very old design at Classic Sailboats, Bethel. (Classic Sailboats, Bethel)*

*Plate 46. **Manx nobby**; "White Heather", built 1904 at Peel, Isle Of Man, has two standing lugsails and two headsails, one connected to the bowsprit end. After a long sailing life the old Manx nobby underwent extensive hull repair and given a new rig at the Watefront Marine boatyard, Porth Penrhyn, to sail again in the 21st century.(Scott Metcalfe, Porth Penrhyn)*

*Plate 47. **Manx Nickie**; this model seen in the Nautical Museum, Castletown, shows how the earlier Manx nickie differed from the later Manx nobby, in Plate 46 in having no bowsprit or headsails, but shared similar characteristics in having two lugsails. (Author)*

Plate 48. ***Dandy smack****; Borth y Gest 1874. In the foreground is a dandy smack with its gaff sail furled, and its mizzen lugsail set on an outrigger, the headsail is furled. The bowsprit is long and fixed. The vessel was used for fishing or cargo carriage due to its large hold. In the background left, a heavily built smack, with its single mast and deep hull is heeling over as it takes the ground.*
(Gwynedd Archives)

Plate 49. ***Sail and steam Porthdinllaen****; from left a steamer, maybe the "Briton", a former sailing barge fitted with a steam engine; then a ketch with its typical curvy topmast, and two smacks.*
(Gwynedd Archives)

Plate 50. ***Ketch****; this Ocean Youth Club ketch, "Sir Francis Drake" is seen anchored off Llaneilian, Anglesey. The club provides transatlantic sailing experience in different vessels with upto ten crew. Despite its modern construction the ketch retains all the essential structural characteristics, with its tall fore mast and shorter mizzen mast, rigged with bermuda type sails. (Author)*

Plate 51. ***Ketch and jigger flats****; seen at Port Dinorwig ; left are two jigger flats, right is a ketch with tall foremast and short mizzen mast. Centre is a two masted topsail schooner, note its deep hull compared to the other cargo carrying vessels. (Milton post card)*

*Plate 52. **Shallop**, model of a shallop at the Nautical Museum, Castletown, Isle Of Man. Note its two tall masts of equal size. The vessel is rigged like a fore -and -aft schooner with a gaff fore sail, a gaff main sail, and a jib. Each gaff sail has two rows of reefing points together with sail battens. The clinker built hull is typically open with a straight stem and transom stern, with thwarts and oars. (Author)*

*Plate 53. **Single topsail schooner**; this lovely single topsail schooner the "Vilma" underway in the Menai Strait, was originally built as a ketch rigged fishing boat in Denmark 1934 and remained as such under different owners until bought in 1996 by Scott Metcalfe. The vessel underwent comprehensive reconstruction at the Waterfront Marine boatyard, Porth Penrhyn and the converted vessel was launched in 2000 as the schooner shown in the picture -possibly the first topsail schooner built and launched in Wales for almost ninety years! (Scott Metcalfe, Porth Penrhyn)*

Plate 54. ***Double topsail schooner****; seen at Porthmadog. The vessel foreground has the typical schooner carvel built hull, the deckhouse is strapped to the deck with iron straps behind it is the freshwater barrel, the stern is a square counter transom. The masts are two part with "crosstrees". Immediately in the background is a larger schooner with a deep hull typical of cargo carriers.*
(National Library Wales)

Plate 55. ***Single topsail schooner****; a plank on frame model of a North American single topsail schooner-known as the Baltimore schooner. Note its curved stem, square stern, and raised quarter deck aft. This type of schooner was used by customs and smugglers, as fast sailing vessels. The bowsprit was 50% of the hull length. The masts are two part. The gaff fore sail is loose footed and the gaff main sail has a boom.*
(Author)

Plate 56. ***Small three masted schooner****; The three masted double topsail topgallant Porthmadog schooner "Gracie", of 96 ton net, built 1907, was one of the smaller vessels. The foremast was two part with "crosstrees", the main and mizzen masts were two part. In this picture she is rigged for fine weather with studding sails to the lower and top foremast, together with a topgallant "moonsail. (Gwynedd Archives)*

Plate 57. ***Large three masted schooner****; The Porthmadog "Dorothy", built 1891, was an example of the larger three masted schooners at 122 ton net, and being typical of Porthmadog three masted schooners had a topgallant sail, and was known as a double topsail standing-topgallant yard schooner. Note her graceful sheerline and steeply steeved bowsprit. (Gwynedd Archives)*

Plate 58. ***Brigantine****; two masted vessel with a three part foremast with a top; fully square rigged; and having a two part mainmast, fully fore-and-aft rigged. This Borth Y Gest built brigantine is the "Edward Windus", 156 ton net, built 1864, lost 1904. (Gwynedd Archives)*

Plate 59. ***Model brigantine;*** *a plank on frame model of a brigantine. Note the three part foremast with its top and "crosstrees", and two part main mast with "crosstrees" only. The upper deck has a quarter deck and focsle deck. The carvel built hull has a straight stem and a square transom stern. (Author)*

Plate 60. ***Brigantine****; the brigantine "Soren Larsen" built 1949, 125 ton net; length 105ft (32m), beam 25. 5ft (7.8m), draft 11.25ft (3.4m). The three part foremast, height 98ft - 29.9m, is fully square rigged, and gaskets are seen along the lower topsail and fore course yards. Buntlines are seen to extend from the squaresail head to the foot. Note the martingale, or dolphin striker, below the bowsprit and the white painted chains of the stays. The vessel has set all her sails in very fine calm weather.*
See also plates 31, 32 and 33.
(Author)

Plate 61. ***Barquentine****; the Portmadoc built barquentine, "Martha Percival", 249 ton net, 1877. This three masted vessel is fully square rigged on its three part foremast with double topsails and single topgallant sails; and fully fore-and-aft rigged on the two part main and mizzen masts.*
(Gwynedd Archives)

*Plate 62. **Barquentine**; The sail training vessel, "Spirit of New Zealand", built through voluntary public subscription for the youth of New Zealand. This beautiful picture shows her in full sail in New Zealand coastal waters, a country with a population equal to that of Wales.*
(Spirit of Adventure Trust NZ)

*Plate 63. **Barquentine**; The sail training vessel "Leeuwin", built through voluntary public subscription for the youth of Western Australia a country with a smaller population, 1. 1 million, than Wales.*
(Sail Training Association of Western Australia)

*Plate 64. **Jack barquentine**; the three masted "Frau Minna Peterson", 165 ton net, was built 1878 in Porthmadog. The vessel was three masted, and all masts were in two parts. The foremast sails included two topsails, and a topgallant sail. No gaff sail present on the foremast, it had a mainmast staysail instead. It was not considered to be a barquentine, neither a three masted topsail schoner-instead it was called a jack barquentine. (Gwynedd Archives)*

*Plate 65. **Three masted schooner**; called the "Jane Banks", this vessel was formerly the jack barquentine "Frau Minna Peterson", see plate 64. It had the rig of a three masted topsail schooner, and its conversion took place in 1901 involving the fitting of the foremast gaff sail instead of the mainmast staysail. Note the absence of the topgallant sail. A jibheaded gaff topsail is on the main mast head. (Gwynedd Archives)*

Plate 66. ***Brig;*** *The Porthmadog brig 'Fleetwing' 226 ton, built 1874. Traded as a phosphate carrier and ended her days as a coal storage hulk in Falkland Islands. Note the double topsail, single topgallant, and the rarely seen royal sail. (Gwynedd Archives)*

Plate 67. ***Brig;*** *The Sea Cadet brig "Royalist", this vessel is fully square rigged on both its masts and has two tops to each mast. The main course is furled. This brig is described as having a single topsail, single topgallant rig. See also plates27 to 30. (Author)*

*Plate 68. **Brig**; The Porthmadog Brig 'Mary Holland', 364 ton, built 1843. Owned by James Baines, Liverpool Black Ball Line, later rebuilt as a 3-masted barque. Lost off Anglesey 1874. Note the single topsail single topgallant rig and rarely set royal. Also the furled crosstack sail. (Gwynedd Archives)*

*Plate 69. **Bark**; the old name is applied to this replica of Captain James Cooks "Endeavour", built 1993. The vessel has three masts, two are fully squared rigged, but the third mast or mizzen is fully fore-and-aft rigged. The fore and main masts are in three parts and have saucer shaped tops, the mizzen has saucer shaped "crosstrees". The hull has a straight stem with bluff bows. A long quarter deck is present. (HM Bark Endeavour Foundation Pty Ltd)*

Plate 70. ***Wooden barque****; the Pwllheli built barque "Koh-i Noor", 303 ton net, 1852, was an example of the small sized barques built in Caernarfonshire. She was sold to Liverpool and ended her days in Tasmania, Australia. (Gwynedd Archives)*

Plate 71. ***Steel barque****; The steel barque "Beeswing", built at Greenock 1901, 1462 ton net, is an example one of the many large barques commanded and crewed by many men from Caernarfonshire.* *See page 112,* *the loss of the steel barque "Friars Crag". Note how the main course is furled and there is a triangular stormsail on the mizzen mast, instead of the full foursided gaff sail. (Gwynedd Archives)*

Plate 72. ***Full rigged ship;*** *a full rigged ship would be fully square rigged on all her masts. This picture shows the FR ship "Riversdale", named after a suburb of Liverpool as were many of the vessels owned by R. W. Leyland of Liverpool. The "Riversdale" was built in Glasgow 1894, ; tonnage 2057 ton net, 275ft(85m) length, 42ft (12. 9m)breadth, and 24. 3ft (7. 5m) depth. It ended its days as a barge in Vancouver Canada. Another example of a large ship commanded and crewed by many men from North Wales. Note how the mizzen course or crossjack sail is furled, also note the triangular mizzen stormsail instead of the foursided gaff sail. (Ceredigion Museum, Coliseum Aberystwyth)*

Plate 73. ***Clipper ship****; the famous "Cutty Sark", a fast sailing ship or clipper, built to carry tea from China. She was built 1869 to outsail the fastest ship of the period, namely the "Thermopylae". Net tonnage 921, just 27 ton less than that of the "Thermopylae. Both were built of wood on iron frames, and had similar dimensions of; 212ft (65m) length, 36ft (11. 05m)breadth, and 21ft(6. 5m) depth. There was a poop deck aft with accommodation for officers below. A skysail could be carried above the royal sails on the main mast, studding sails were also carried. (Nautical Photo Agency)*

PEOPLE

Plate 74. ***Captain Robert Hugh Jones*** *(1868 -1892), of Croeshigol House, Trefor, schoonerman, master mariner square rig, chief officer of the steel barque "Friars Crag" – lost with all hands 1892 off east coast of Australia.*
(Dafydd Williams)

Plate 75. ***Richard Tudor****, of Pwllheli; sailmaker, educator, ocean yachtsman skipper, master in sail, twice round the world circumnavigator.*
(Author)

Plate 76. ***Shipmates****; Maritime historians, authors, educators, and former RN seamen, the late Aled Eames, and Frank Rhys Jones; together with the author aboard the brigantine "Soren Larsen", during a Jubilee Sailing Trust sponsored voyage 1984.*
(Christopher Rudd)

Plate 77. ***Mici Plwm****, of Llan Ffestiniog, electrician, television actor and entertainer, author, and deepwater yachtsman; at the wheel of the brigantine "Soren Larsen", together with veteran JST ocean sailor Hywel Williams of Llanaber.* *(Author)*

Plate 78. ***Voyage Crew****; aboard the brigantine "Soren Larsen" 1984, include shipmates from Llanuwchlyn, Dyffryn Ardudwy, Bangor, Glyn Ceiriog and Dolgellau.* *(Author)*

Plate 79. ***Glyn Heddwyn Jones*** *(1954-2007); of Cwm Prysor, Trawsfynydd; hill farmer, cane craft worker, choir member, and a very happy and proficient sailor, aboard the brigantine "Soren Larsen" – 1984.* *(Author)*

Plate 80. ***Deckscene;*** *Aboard brig 'Evelyn', 216 ton, built Porthmadog 1877, lost 1916. Looking forward note the cabin companions, and freshwater barrel abaft main mast. The dolly winch next to master and dog, with boat and galley behind. the 'W.C.' is near starboad rail behind man with bucket.*
(Gwynedd Archives)

Plate 81. ***Careening;*** *A schooner has been heeled over by hauling on masts or shifting ballast in order to repair the hull keel.*
(Gwynedd Archives)

*Plate 82. **Jack barquentine;** The 'C.E. Spooner', 172 to, built Porthmadog 1878, as a jack barquentine. Note: the staysail furled instead of a gaff foresail. No single mast is square rigged. All masts are two part. (Gwynedd Archives)*

*Plate 83. **Ketch;** A ketch underway with furled gaff mizzen and jib sails, crossing Porthmadog estuary, with the 'Cwch Bach' astern. (Gwynedd Archives)*

Plate 84. ***Topsail schooner****; 'The Oaklets', 147 ton, built Porthmadog 1892. Picture taken prior to her maiden voyage. Lost in Mediterranean on her second voyage, 1893. (Gwynedd Archives)*

Plate 85. ***Topsail schooner****; The 'Dorothy' (I), 142 ton, built Porthmadog 1891. A Newfoundland trader. Lost 1905.*

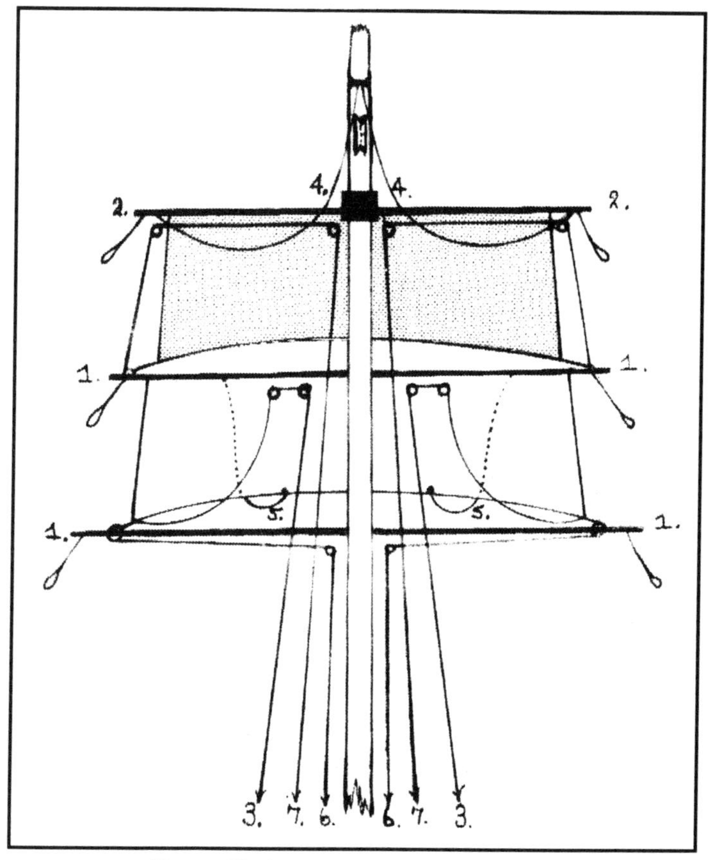

Figure 60. Squaresail, running rigging.

Other sailing vessel machines include; capstans, winches, windlasses, pumps, and oars, all operated by *man-power* in the early sailing vessels.

Square Sail Yard Running Rigging. See Figure 59.

- The running rigging moves the yards when working a ship.
- Square sail yards are either *standing*; or *hoisting* yards.

Standing yards, are crossed to the mast and *fixed* by truss bands, see Plate 25; whilst, *hoisting yards* see Figure 59, are crossed to the mast by parrals (parrels) (1), which allow the yard to *slide* up and down the mast (2). (Note; some steel masted ships do not have parrals, instead the yards slide up and down tracks by means of shoes)

• *Braces* connect with the yardarms by way of blocks and the brace pendants (3), they *square* the yards or move them horizontally during *bracing*.

• *Lifts* (4) connect with the yardarms to the mast to support and steady the yard, and can be adjusted to make the yard slope, or to make them *cock billed*, when alongside a quay or dock which is also used as a sign of mourning respect.

• *Standing lifts*, (4) Figure 60, *usually* hang down abaft of the sail when the yard is raised and the sail is set; they are taut when the the yard is lowered and the sail is furled.

• *Yard halliards or* haulyards, hoist the movable yards, through the following system shown in Figure 59 and its inset.

• The *tye* (5) is a chain connecting with centre, or slings, of a yard and roves through a *sheave* (6) in the mast, and hence to a *tye block* (7).

The standing part of the halliard (8) is fixed to the ship rail and roved through the tye block to the *halliard tackle or gin tackle* (9) composed of two blocks, the lower one is connected to the ship rail.

The upper block has it *halliard lead* rove through the *lead block* (10) and emerges as the *halliard fall* (11), or loose end, which is hauled on by the crew accompanied usually by a *halliard shanty*.

• Also shown in the figure is the jackstay (12) to which the sail head is bent by means of robands, and the *footrope* (13) for crew to stand on.

Square Sail Running Rigging See Figure 60.

The square sail running rigging serves to move the square sails when working ship.

The Figure 60 is a very simplified diagram showing a *standing* yard (1) and *hoisting* yard (2) and their square sails, together with the following running rigging lines;

• *Clew lines* (3) haul up the the lower outer corners of the square sails to their standing yards yards during sail furling.

The Figure 60 is a view from *abaft* the sail.

- *Buntlines* (5) haul up the middle lower part or sail foot to the standing yards during sail furling; they are seen from the forward side of the sail in Plates 33, 60, 63 and 72.
- *Sheets* (6) connect with the sail lower corner or clews and are hauled during setting the sails.
- *Downhauls* (7) haul down the movable yard during sail furling or when shortening sail.
- *Bowlines* keep the sail leech taut.
- *Leech lines* gather and control the sail leeches when furling.
- The standing lifts (4) are slack when the sail is set or when the yard is hoisted; and taut when the yard is lowered and the sail furled.

Belaying Gear

Running rigging lines are belayed or fastened to belaying pins, or cleats, by twining around without seizing, thus allowing the line to be released easily and quickly.

- *Pin rails* are racks for the belaying pins arranged inside the bulwarks of a ships side. See Plates 23 and 24.
- *Spider bands* hold belaying pins and are attached to the lower part of the lower mast.
- *Fife rails* encircle the foot of the mainmast and the pump, and hold the belaying pins. See Plate 79
- *Bitts* and samson posts, are upright frames of strong timber in the fore and after parts of the deck and serve to belay the heavier anchor cables, and also the fore braces and topsail sheets. See Plates 11, 17 and 18.
- *Cavills,* kevils or kavils, are large cleats to belay the main braces, sheets and tacks. See Plate 19 and 20.

Shanties

Shanties are songs sung to accompany various sailing ship operations. A variety exist in Welsh and English only one has been given as an an example in the following.

- Forebitters are sung around the fore bitts during idle times – "Nelly Dean".
- Halliard shanties for hauling on the halliards – "Blow the Man Down".

- Sheet shanties for hauling the fore and main sheets "Haulaway Joe".
- Capstan shanties for the tacks, sheets, clews, and anchor – "Rio Grande".
- Stamp and go or walk away shanties for manning the braces, capstan, hawsers and halliards – "Drunken Sailor".
- Sweating up or swigging off, shanties to pull at a rope with a jerking action using body weight – "Heave and bust her".

A Pwllheli Slave Trader

The *Mary* built 1801 in Pwllheli, of 437 tons, was sold to Forbes and Co and J. Bolton of Liverpool. The hull had been sheathed with copper in order to prevent fouling by marine crustaceans in tropical waters, and according to Lloyds Register she was trading in Liberia, West Africa, in 1803 and 1804. Locally in Pwllheli she was known to be a "guineaman" – a term for a negro slave ship able to carry upto 600 slaves.

Fast Clipper Ships. Plates 71, 72 and 73

Fast sailing ships had existed since the time of the cutter and American schooner. In Britain the fast fully square rigged sailing ships, flourished from the 1850s to 1870s following the revolution in hull design which originated in Aberdeen at the Alexander Hall shipyard about 1840. This shipyard designed the famous clipper bow called the *Aberdeen bow,* Figure 61, this together with other hull improvements lead to improved speed of the fast sailing or clipper ships such as: schooners, barques, and full rigged ships-and ultimately the fastest sailing ship of her time the *Thermopylae* built also in Aberdeen by Walter Hood & Co.

The full rigged ship *Mimosa* which carried Welsh emigrants to Patagonia in 1865, was built by Alexander Hall in Aberdeen in 1853, and had an Aberdeen bow typical of a fast sailing ship.

Figureheads

Almost one third of all the sailing vessels built in Caernarfonshire during the period 1750 to 1913 had some

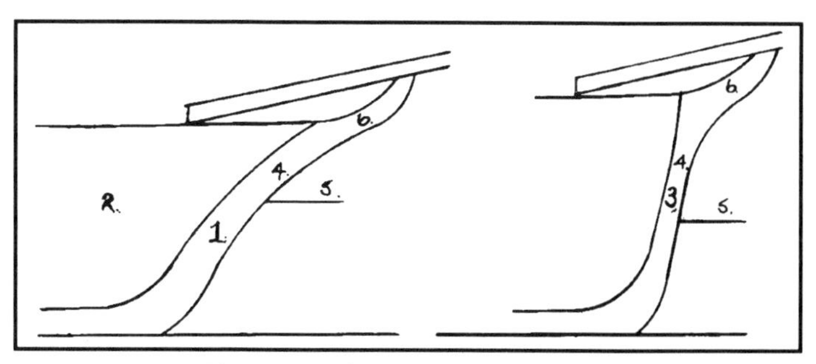

Figure 61. The Aberdeen bow (left).

sort of *stem post head* ornamentation or a figurehead.

Cutters, wherries, shallops, dandies, flats and galliots were without a figurehead, and a very small minority of sloops, ketches and smacks were built with a *figurehead*.

All other vessel types: FR ships, barques, brigantines, barquentines, brigs, snows, and three masted schooners were built with a figurehead. Approximately 80% of the two masted schooners had a figurehead.

The figurehead appeared in early maritime history on the stem and stern post heads of the Scandinavian vessels; mainly as dragon heads: whilst the Roman cargo vessels had a swan figure at the stern post head with a simple form or design at the stem head. Cogs were without figure heads, whilst the carrack and galleons, man-of-war and merchantmen had a figurehead at the end of the beak.

Figure 61 shows the stem post structure being composed of the *cutwater* (4) near the water line (5), with the *stem post knee* above (6), known by oldtime shipwrights as "the knee of the head". The carved figurehead would be fixed by bolts into the stem post knee head. Apart from supporting the figurehead the stem post knee would also partly support the bowsprit.

Three main types of figurehead occurred in Caernarfonshire vessels:

a) *family* figureheads – of men, women, and children, were typical of 88% of Caernarfonshire vessels. The figurehead could be half size, or bosom figures, or full length figures. They would represent the ships name

or owners family.
Caernarfon and Porth Dinllaen figureheads were 60-65% female; whilst Pwllheli, Porthmadog, Nefyn, Bangor, Y Felinheli and Conwy figureheads were 60-80% male. The human form implied its living connection with the "living"vessel which was essentialy female.
The female bosom figurehead may have been descended from the knarr Scandinavian bow, which was described as bosomy with good sailing qualities in its bluff or breastlike bow. Exposed bare breasts on the figurehead were supposed to calm storms!

b) *animal* figureheads amounted to 2% of all vessels; appeared as eagles, swans, bird beaks, three feathers, and goats.
c) *ornamental* figureheads amounted to 8% of all vessels and included; *fiddle* heads curling inwards to the stem post head; *scroll* heads curling outwards; and *billet* heads resembling a wave curving in and out. A simple unadorned form was called the knee of the head, as shown in the Figure 61.

Figureheads from wrecks were often to be found in Llŷn fixed to the exterior walls of farmhouses.

Vessel Names

The majority of vessel names in Caernarfonshire were English. Welsh names were in a very small minority and were mainly for place names, or names for animals.

Female names were given to over 50% of all the vessels names, maintaining the connotation that a sailing vessel or any other watercraft, was female, and also in the way it was was described as a "she" or "her".

Male names were popular to the extent of 16% of the total vessels and included those of; families, shipowners, landowners, shipbuilders, merchants, and clergymen.

Both sexes were also used as names in a small minority of 2% of the total: for example as *John & Ellen, John & Ann,* and *John & Mary.*

Virtues: or qualities were popular to the extent of over 13% of all the vessels named, for example: *Silence, Integrity,*

Prosperity, Humility, Love and *Celerity.*

Place names: ranked at over 8% of total and were mainly Welsh: *Isallt, Snowdonia, Merioneth, Nefyn* and *Great Britain.*

Animals including birds, amounted to about 5% of the total and included: *Osprey, Eagle, Fly, Bee* and *Whale.*

The remaining names which formed about 3% of the total, included stars: *Morning Star* and *Venus*: gems, *Emerald* and *Ruby*; and a few plants such as *Vine* and *Heather Bell.*

Fast Sailing Ship Hull Features. Plates 71, 72 and 73.

The fast full rigged sailing ships appeared after 1850.

The characteristics of the fast sailing ship hull, which was capable of over 9 knots or upto 18 knots in favourable conditions, were briefly as follows;

a) a fine lined streamlined hull with a sharp end.

b) a raked stem (1), shown in Figure 61 together with a long entry (2), composing the Aberdeen bow. The bow is shown compared to the old style straight and vertical stem (3) with bluff bows.

c) the hull body was rounded with a large deadrise.

d) a low freeboard and shallow draught.

e) a raked stern together with a rounded stern and counter.

f) a L/B ratio of more than five.

Square Sail Rig Development to 1900.

Apart from hull development, the second factor in the search for speed was the increase in total *sail area,* this could be achieved by increasing the number of masts and their heights, or the total area of the *normal* sails, courses, topsails topgallants and royals. Or by adding *flying kites,* sails set high on the masts as *skysails,* with *moonsails* above; they were of little real value and set only in fine weather. The ultimate result was to produce a very *tall* vessel.

The most effective method of increasing sail area was by means of *studding sails* or stunsails (1) shown in Figure 62; they were set outside the normal square sails, and spread out at the foot by *studding sail booms* (2), which slid outward along the yardarms. The studding sail head was extended by *studding sail yards* (3). Lower studding sails were extended by

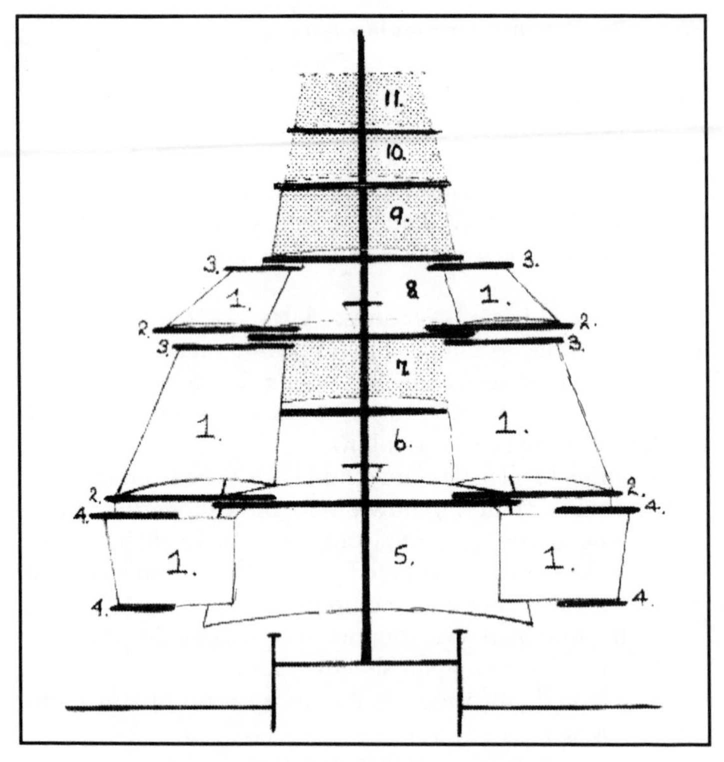

Figure 62. A full rigged ship of 1870s.

battens (4). Studding sails were discontinued during the 1870s.

The progressive change in the square sail rig composition took place from before 1800 to 1890 and mainly involved the topsails and topgallant sails, and royal sails. The courses, headsails, staysails, and gaff sails were involved to a lesser extent.

The square sail rig development is related to the periods: pre-1850, 1850-1870, 1870-1890, and post-1890, these periods in turn were affected by hull design development, and prevailing economic conditions, mainly in availability of manpower.

a) **Pre 1850** sail rig: **single topsails** and **single topgallant sails** with **royal sails** – see Figure 58. The

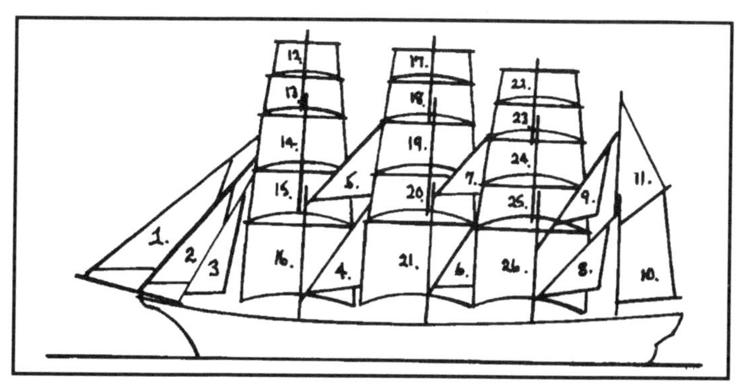

Figure 63. A baldheaded barque of the 1930s..

full rigged ships built in Caernarfonshire were of this period and sail rig. See also Figures: 51, 52 (a), 56 and 57 (a).

b) **1850 to 1870** sail rig: **double topsails** and **single topgallant sails** with **royal sails**. This rig was typical of the fast sailing ships: *Thermopylae* and *Cutty Sark.* See Plate 73. (Later in the 1870s the *Thermopylae* had double topgallant sails fitted).
See also Figures 55, and 57 (b).

c) **1870 to 1890** sail rig: **double topsails** and **double topgallant sails** with **royal sails** and **flying kites**. This rig was typical of the fast tea, wool, and passenger clipper ships and is shown in Figure 62; it is composed of; lower topsail (6) and upper topsail (7): lower top gallant sail (8) and upper top gallant sail (9); with royal sail (10) and skysail (11).
The sails shown shaded in Figure 62; sails (7), (9), (10), and (11) are bent to *hoisting* yards. Sails (5), (6) and (8), are bent to *standing* fixed yards.

d) **Post 1890** sail rig; **double topsails** and **double topgallant** sails only.

Known as the *stump topgallant* or *baldheaded rig,* it had no sails above the topgallants. See Plates 71 and 72.

Figure 63 shows the typical sail rig of a stump topgallant, or baldheaded, four masted barque that was afloat during the 1930s. This rig was economical in crew, fewer men were needed to work fewer square sails; the barque having fewer square sails than a similar masted FR sailing ship. Consequently barques were favoured by owners of general trading vessels and during the final years of sail they were the "work-horses", or cargo carriers, with low freight charges.

The sail rig of the four-mast barque in Figure 63 is composed as follows:

a) *headsails*: outer jib (1), inner jib (2), and fore topmast staysail (3).

b) *mast staysails*: main topmast staysail (4), main topgallant staysail (5), mizzen topmast staysail (6), mizzen topgallant staysail (7), jigger staysail (8), and jigger topmast staysail (9).

c) *gaff sails*: gaff sail, or spanker (10), and jib-headed gaff topsail (11).

d) *square sails:*

The four masts are named: foremast, main mast, mizzen mast and *jigger* mast.

• Fore mast: fore upper topgallant sail (12), fore lower topgallant sail (13), fore upper topsail (14), fore lower topsail (15), and fore course, or foresail (16).

• Main mast: main upper topgallant sail (17), main lower topgallant sail (18), main upper topsail (19), main lower topsail (20), and main course, or main sail (21).

• Mizzen mast: mizzen upper topgallant sail (22), mizzen lower topgallant sail (23), mizzen upper topsail (24), mizzen lower topsail (25), and mizzen course or crossjack sail ((26).

Many FR sailing ships were converted into barques by removing the square sails from the mizzen or jigger masts. A careful examination of paintings and pictures of square rigged sailing vessels will disclose the type of rig and indicate the age and period of the vessel.

Future Wind Power Transport

It is almost a hundred years since the last wooden sailing vessel was built in Caernarfonshire. It was a mode of sea transport displaced by the fossil fuel burning steamships and motor ships. Today there is a major concern for the reduction of carbon dioxide emissions and the dwindling supply of non-renewable fossil fuels; these factors are having a known effect on the climate. The search for alternative renewable energy sources has seen the introduction of solar power, and wind power energy generation, and any other means which does not harm the environment.

Wind powered sailing vessels have been tried and proved over hundreds of years as an efficient non-polluting means of transport, originally used in world discovery and in establishing world trade routes. It is clearly evident that the present time and environmental conditions will facilitate the return of the modern sailing vessel.

The modernised powered sailing vessel will provide a means of transport with reduced energy costs, free from the environmental pollution of; heat, noise, chemical smog and absolutely clear of any carbon dioxide emission.

Now is the time to reopen, or enlarge, our shipyards, and to reintroduce new shipbuilding skills, together with methods of sail training for crewing these modernised wind powered transport vessels of the immediate future. A vital regeneration of a former means of sea transport which should be an essential part of the future carbon-free transport policy of the Assembly of Wales.

Cymru a'r Môr articles include:
"O Bwllheli i ben draw y byd", Aled Eames; Vol 25, 2004.
"Personal chapter *Monkbarns*", J.Ifor Davies, Vol 2, 1977.
"The *Cardigan Castle*,1870-1907" G. Hawkes, Vol 16, 1994.

16. HWYL CYMRU - SAIL WALES

Wales is a maritime mountainous country and has a coastline of nearly one thousand miles with most of its population located on the coast, and inland places no more than fifty miles away from the sea. For centuries the coastal area has supported and provided a way of life related to the sea and contributed to the identity of this small nation mentioned in our National Anthem: "Tra môr yn fur i'r bur hoff bau –". More than half the population of this maritime country face the sea each day and look upon it with mixed feelings of affection for its different moods, or with sadness for taking away loved ones that have gone abroad and others who never returned from voyages.

An attempt has been made in the previous pages of this book to describe the maritime heritage of Caernarfonshire – a county which mirrors the rest of Wales – a sea girt county. A county with a rich past tradition of shipbuilding and seafaring, which has become a fond memory with hardly a relic of its glorious maritime heritage to be seen. But once a square rigged sailing vessel is spied on the coast, or berthing alongside the quay, the Caernarfonshire people turn out in droves drawn by the inborne affection for all things maritime and the family bonds linked to their seafaring ancestors. Eager to see the beauty of sail, or tread the decks, of a sailing ship, the like of which that Taid, or someone else, owned or sailed on through mighty seas, to the ends of the Earth – "I ben draw y byd".

Despite the disappearance of the Welsh sailing ship into the mists of time during the last century, the immortality of the sailing ship remains elsewhere and is the immediate concern of over 17 maritime nations worldwide who have seen the decline of their sailing fleet. Fearful that their hard won maritime heritage would disappear for ever, these nations during the last fifty years have made headway in restoring their heritage in sail through building and crewing *sail training* or *sail adventure* ships. These vessels are their nations flag-ships, proudly flying the flag and displaying their national identity in ports throughout the world, or at the annual tall ships gatherings. In addition these maritime countries are preparing for the regeneration of alternative means of transport for a future of reduced oil fuel supplies.

Countries worldwide are providing their youth with the opportunity to restore their pride in the maritime past history by sailing in the square rigged sailing ships. A generation is reaching out to touch and is reliving the experience of what their forebears did also under sail, which brought them to their colonial homes, or in discovering new worlds. Amongst these nations are small countries with populations *smaller* than Wales who have been operating sail training vessels for more than twenty years. For example;

a) **Western Australia** (popn 1.01 million) – Leeuwin Ocean Adventure – Fremantle, built the three masted barquentine the *Leeuwin*, 165ft (50m) during 1983, – Plate 63, and it was sailing in 1986 carrying forty young people with a fulltime crew of six. At one time the Captain was a Welshspeaking Welshman! Anyone, including those with certain health limitations are also able to join the voyages. The ship is operated by a private non-profit organisation. Website: www. leeuwin. com

b) **New Zealand** (popn – 2.86 million) – Spirit of Adventure Trust, Auckland, started in 1973 by building the brigantine *Spirit Of Adventure* 108ft (33.1m), mainly by means of a private donation, and have since built a replacement, the barquentine *The Spirit of New Zealand* 148ft (45.4m), Plate 62. The Trust has carried over 50000 trainees during their 30 years of existence on voyages around the New Zealand coast. From time to to time disabled trainees are carried and special voyages are provided for adults. Website www. spiritofadventure. org. nz

c) **Eire** (popn 2.8 million) started with the brigantine *Asgard 2*, 99ft (30.4m), in 1981, owned by Coiste an Asgard, has a fulltime crew of five and carries twenty trainees on voyages of 2 weeks around the Irish coast and worldwide. During a voyage off the west coast of Australia, Bass Strait, between Tasmania and New South Wales, in January 1988, a medical crew member, and founder, of the STS *Leeuwin* was transferred to the STS *Asgard 2* to treat an injured member of the Irish crew. What a wonderful meeting of two sail training ships! What an example of friendship stretching across oceans! Website: www. asgard2 ie.

Sail Training Objectives

Those who promote and operate sail training ships say that the main objective is to provide an experience of a component of the environment, ie the sea, which covers 75 % of the earths surface. The aspects of this experience are:

Physically in working the ship, being tired, wet, cold and maybe sick, in enjoying suns warmth, the fresh salty air, and the feel of the wind. Roughing it in a changing environment of calm and storm, away from the steady environment of home. To feel the wheels kick, and hear the smack of the sails.

Mentally to accept boredom, sudden change, to be frightened and excited, to have fun, to accept discipline.

Socially to understand others, their strengths and weaknesses, to accept challenges and integrate, and to discover ones own hidden abilities, and broaden the social outlook, and acquire self respect. To learn leadership, or just be a small part of a big team working together in a very small environment from which nobody can walk away.

Appreciating the beauty of the sea in all its moods, the beauty of the sail, and the silent passage of the ship through the sea, the star studded night sky, and the scudding clouds. To be as one with the ship and share a love for it, and the loneliness of it all.

In all a rare life experience from which young people emerge stimulated having accepted challenges unknown in a life ashore, and having met with others as strangers come away as shipmates.

Shipboard Activities

Shipboard activities occupy almost every hour from, being called out at some unearthly hour, to the time one gets ones head down in a bunk or hammock. The main activity is learning to work the ship as a team, in acquiring ship operating skills, working the sails either aloft or below on deck, and altogether on a rope at the Mate's orders. Standing watches night and day, on lookout in the bow, or at the helm watching the course, or quietly yarning together over a mug of tea or coffee in the dark night, ever watchful for the safety of the ship. Cleaning out the berths, the galley and the heads. Shanty singing and visits ashore, and the pleasure of ship visiting to other sailing ships in port, of arriving in new places – and the total sadness of leaving her!

Sail for Wales – Hwyl i Gymru

Having outlined the thriving existence of sail training vessels across the world, the reality of a similar sailing ship for Wales is within the bounds of possibility in this affluent age, which contrasts with Welsh shipbuilding ventures of 200 years ago. The small seafaring communities throughout Wales built their own chapels and ships in a way that was a standing tradition – something that could be done again in this age when our forebears efforts of chapel building and ship-building has turned to demolition and decay.

The old sailing ships were built for carriage of slates, fruits, coal, timber and sadly slaves – a new sailing ship for Wales would be built for the carriage of youth to revive the spirit of the past and replicate the characters of their forebears – who no longer would be part of a family history but a living continuation.

The principal objective would be to build ONE sailing ship for Wales. One vessel to be a mirror image and to regenerate the past. Something active and alive, from construction to sailing. Not a static memorial or a museum object, something involving active participation, and certainly *not* a spectator past-time which fills our sports arenas and stadiums.

Finance

The raising of the essential werewithall has proved no problem in the building of sail training ships elsewhere. Other nations have readily, and proudly, found the sources and have maintained their vessel upkeep, fulltime crew, and have even built another vessel.

Devolultion has brought us awareness of nationhood and the Welsh Assembly should provide encouragement and support for a wind powered sailing project. The Assembly has yet to respond fully to the challenge to take up *wind power* as an alternative to *fossil fuel power*. The greatest environmental source of CO^2 comes from fossil fuel powered *transport*. A means of reducing this environmental pollution would be by establishing *sail training* in Wales to prepare for a future of *wind powered sailing vessels* – a zero carbon means of transport, using an alternative and renewable energy source-the wind for free!

To this extent the Assembly could have a *maritime transport section* within its structure, concerned with wind powered sailing vessels their economics, construction, manning and training all aimed as part of the process to move Wales from a carbon intensive economy. This is a national responsibility and should *not* be left to charitable causes.

County Council subscription to the National Eisteddfod typifies that the same can apply to a ship for Wales, and stimulation of a county's maritime heritage. The bards have for long sung the praises of our maritime past – now is the time to activate the dream.

Public subscriptions have built sail training ships, and a "pound a head of the population fund" for Wales could raise at least £3 million, supplemented by annual collections and local branch subscriptions. The Merchant Shipping Act of 1824 specified ship shares should be made up of sixty four shares – a smaller share of *one three millionth* from everyone in Wales would meet the cost amply!

Private donations from bequests or outright donations from worthies and notables at home and abroad, are typical of what other countries have done. A major Welsh donor could even *name the vessel!*

Industrial donations from those *depleting* our maritime non-renewable coastal resources should figure prominently. Similarly windpower harnessers scattered around our coast can donate as fellow users of a renewable environmental energy source.

Ship Construction

The alternatives of ship construction are-self build, or to build to order by a shipyard.

The Jubilee Sailing Trust ordered a barque called the *Lord Nelson,* and having been so successful, the Trust have now built their own *Tenacious* by DIY-many volunteers from everywhere, including Wales, went to spend a residential week putting a plank in the sailing ship!

The Welsh ship could be built replicating shipbuilding methods as performed on the shores of Wales in the past, or on the slipway at the Porth Penrhyn yard, which could be used later for overhaul and maintenance. The Plate 16 shows the STS *Leeuwin* undergoing construction in much the same place as ships were built on the shores of Nefyn, Porth Dinllaen, Pwllheli and Trefor.

Caernarfonshire today is fortunate in having thriving small ship and boat building yards together with a workforce at Classic Sailboats, Bethel and Waterfront Marine at Porth Penrhyn, Bangor. Traditional wooden vessels can be built here from rowing boats, cutters, to topsail schooners upto 70ft (22m), and old vessels can be reconstructed. In the main local renewable resources of timber are being used.

Scott Metcalfe of Porth Penrhyn Boatyard has kindly

submitted the following drawing of his idea of a sail training and adventure vessel for Sail Wales – Hwyl Cymru. It embodies a three masted topgallant schooner of the type built in Porthmadog during the early 1900s. This vessel would be able to undertake coastal voyages and in having a shallow draft it could enter most of the smallest port and harbours in Wales, and in so doing bring this Welsh schooner to the people in every coastal part of Wales. This type of vessel would be capable of making transatlantic voyages in the tradition of the old Porthmadog Western Ocean yachts.

Modern shipbuilding skills and technology have eclipsed the old methods and a workforce could be found and trained, and supplemented by a *Welsh marine school*, such as exists in Falmouth, for traditional shipbuilding skills.

Links

The strong existing maritime services of Wales include:

The Urdd with sailing facilities at Bala and Llangrannog.

The Outward Bound school at Aberdovey-started by two who believed in sail training as character forming-Kurt Hahn and Lawrence Holt. Over 3500 young people have attended the school to sail and row in dinghies and cutters. Plas Menai Sailing centre has sail training in a variety of sailing vessels.

Ocean Youth Club at Holyhead operate a ketch, Plate 50, which has taken many young people from Wales at their own expense on coastal and transatlantic voyages.

Sea Cadets in many parts of Wales, provide sail training through the brig *Royalist*. See Plate 67

The Jubilee Sailing Trust provides offshore sailing for disabled and able bodied crews – and have supporting branches in Wales.

Bangor University Dept of Oceanography operate the *Prince Madog* marine research vessel, which could liaise with a wind powered sailing vessel.

Marinas in Caernarfon, Conwy, Deganwy, Porthmadog, Porth Dinorwig, Pwllheli, Holyhead can can be a source of enrolment, recruitment, and cooperation, also a means of berthing the vessel.

Operational Area

The main area would be the whole coast of Wales with the vessel calling regularly at all ports and harbours to show the flag, recruit trainees, and deliver *freight*. The vessel would travel the *Welsh maritime highway*, unrestricted by congestion, and show how the the seaway is a nonpolluting freeway for transport, a means which the National Assembly could well support and investigate.

Overnight and daytime voyages between North and South Wales could be made on a regular basis. A speedier and healthier means of transport than by the present archaic road system.

The **Celtic Sea voyages** would be to the Celtic Nations to establish and strengthen links – the coasts of Eire, the Western Isles of Scotland, Isle of Man, Cornwall, Channel Islands, Brittany and the Iberian coast.

A renenactment voyage of the *Mimosa* to Patagonia, or transatlantic voyage to Newfoundland in the tradition of the "Western Ocean Yachts" of Porthmadog, would be a crowning achievment, hopefully skippered by Caernarfonshire's master in sail, and twice world ocean circumnavigator, Skipper Richard Tudor of Pwllheli. Plate 75.

Crewing – Has it been done?

YES! and absolutely no problems with total enjoyment by all! During 1984, Aled Eames the former seaman, educator, eminent maritime historian, tv presenter and author, together with Frank Rhys Jones, former headmaster, seaman and ship preservationist and myself, Plate 76, sailed aboard the brigantine *Soren Larsen* from Southampton to Channel Islands. The nature of this trip was to promote the formation of a north Wales branch of the Jubilee Sailing Trust. During the voyage the idea of a sailing ship for Wales was discussed, Aled and Frank believed Wales had a rich maritime and proud tradition to realise this notion for the youth of Wales.

Later in 1984 Mici Plwm, Plate 77, the well known tv actor, entertainer, writer and offshore sailor, organised an appeal for disabled people from Wales to sail aboard the brigantine *Soren Larsen* Plate 60 – the appeal had a massive and immediate response with sufficient being collected for two cruises. Amongst the first to join was Glyn Heddwyn Jones of Cwm Prysor, Trawsfynydd, Plate 79, a former hill farmer, and skilled craftsman in woven canework, who lost his sight at the age of 25 years. Despite having the severe disability of blindness, Glyn proved to be an extremely keen sailor and topman, having climbed upto the yards on more than one occasion. He was always eager to take his trick at the wheel, and excelled as a helmsman during the dark night watches. Sadly this ever smiling and cheerful sailor passed away May 11th, 2007, and will always be remembered as a founder crewman of sail training in Wales.

The first cruise was Swansea to Liverpool calling at Caernarfon and Irish ports, the second cruise was Liverpool to Swansea calling at Moelfre, Beaumaris, and Wicklow.

The voyage crews, see Plate 78, came from: Swansea, Llwyndyrus, Porthmadog, Blaenau Ffestiniog, Mynytho, Dolgellau, Talysarn, Llandecwyn, Cardiff, Trawsfynydd, Bala, Bangor, Dyffryn Ardudwy, Old Colwyn, Colwyn Bay, Penisarwaen, Aberystwyth, Pwllheli, Harlech and Llanberis – a sample sufficient to demonstrate the wide Welsh interest.

During the time the brigantine *"Soren Larsen"* was berthed in Caernarfon, hundreds of "pobl y môr" turned up in torrential rain to look the ship over. One particular visitor was Hywel Williams of Llanaber, age 16 at the time, whose great grandfather was Master of the three masted schooner *Donald and Doris* built 1897 in Amlwch, Anglesey. To cut a long yarn short and to show the determination of a youngster to sail aboard a sailing ship – Hywel has regularly sailed every year, for over 22 years in the sailing ships of the Jubilee Sailing Trust – emulating his seafaring ancestors who would be justly proud of him – no mean achievement for one who has never walked and did it all from a wheelchair. See Plate 77.

Hywel is symbolic of so many of the youth of Wales, able bodied or disabled, who given the chance and the means, would launch a sailing ship for Wales tomorrow, and sail aboard her as *ambassadors* and *champions* to promote Wales worldwide.

GLOSSARY

Abaft; towards the stern.
Afore; towards the bow.
Acockbill; or cockbilled, a yard slewed at an angle to the mast, or a hanging anchor at the cathead.
Artemon; a small square sail set on a deeply steeved artemon mast, in the bows of early Roman vessels.
Athwart; across the vessels hull.
Adze; a shipwright carpenters tool for chipping wood.
Backstays; the aftermost stays of a mast.
Bag-o-wrinkle; or puddening, is old ropeyarn used to prevent rigging chafing the sails.
Baldheaded; is a vessel without her normal topmast spars, or without sail above the upper topgallant.
Beak; a projection of the forepart of galleons and other early vessels, used as a ram. The beakhead was a small deck ahead of the forecastle.
Beam; the width of a vessel, or deck supports.
Beitass; a spar stretching the sail edge in Viking vessels.
Belay; to make fast a running rope, without seizing or hitching.
Belaying, pins; in racks to make fast the running rigging.
Bend; to fasten sails to yards, or ropes together.
Billboard; a board at the bow to prevent anchor bills damaging the hull.
Billhead; a carving at the vessels stem head.
Bilge; or bulge, is the turn between the hull bottom and the vessels sides, and is the part on which the vessel rests when it takes the ground. Water collects inside the hull at the bilge.
Bitts; strong vertical timbers coming up through the decks to belay anchor cables. Bitts are found either side of a windlass.
Block; is a pulley used in running rigging.
Boat; is a small vessel.
Bobstays; are stays which hold the bowsprit end downwards towards the stem.
Bolsters; are soft material on the trestletrees, on which the eyes of the mast rigging rest.
Bolt ropes; are fastened round the edges of sails.
Bonaventure; the fourth mast in a carrack which carries a lateen sail.
Boom; is the is the spar at the foot of a fore and aft sail, or studding sail.

Bowline; a rope which holds the leech of a square sail well forward.
Bowsprit; boltsprit, a spar projecting over the vessels bow.
Braces; lines or ropes used to move the yards about.
Brails; are ropes which gather spritsails, standing gaffsails, and trysails to the mast.
Bulwarks; the sides of a vessel above the upper deck, and consist of boards fixed to stanchions and timber heads.
Bumpkin; a short stumplike iron bowsprit in open boats taking a foresail, also a horizontal spar projecting over the stern taffrail in a dandy smack or yawl, called an outrigger or jigger boom.
Bunt; is the middle part of a square sail.
Buntlines; haul up the lower middle part of the square sail when furling.
Burden, burthen; the capacity of a vessel in tuns or tons.
Cable; is a large strong rope fastened to the anchor.
Capping; covers the top of the bulwarks.
Camber; the curve of a vessels deck.
Cap; connects the lower mast head with the lower part of the upper mast, in a masthead assembly. A similar cap is found betwen the bowsprit and jibboom spars.
Capping; is the top of the bulwarks.
Capstan; a vertical anchor weighing machine used mainly in naval men-of-war.
Caulking; a filling between planks.
Carvel; the planks are flush-laid edge to edge, providing the hull with a smooth exterior.
Cat; is the tackle used to hoist the anchor.
Catheads; Plate 26, are located in the bows of sailing vessels to hold the anchor, before letting go or securing on the anchor bed after weighing.
Cavil; or kevel, are horizontal timbers connected to the bulwark stanchions, which function to belay heavy ropes.
Ceiling; (sealing) the planks lining a hold or vessel.
Chafing, gear – see bag-o-wrinkle.
Chains; are the channels and chain plates outside the hull which take the shrouds in a sailing vessel.
Cheeks; fixed to lower masthead hounds, support the trestletrees of the masthead assembly.
Clench; or clinch, is the method of fastening timbers together with nail, rivets and roves.
Clew; is the after lower corner of a fore and aft sail, or the lower corners of a square sail.
Clew lines; are ropes which lift clews of the upper square sails to their yard bunt or centre, or to their yardarms.

Clew up; to haul up the square sails with clewlines and buntlines prior to furling.
Clinker; the method of laying planks so they overlap at the edges to produce a roughened outer hull surface. The old term was clencher, or clench built. Consequently, the terms, clinker, clincher, clencher are synonymous for a clench built hull; these terms contrast with the American lapstrake and shiplap. Clinker is the term currently preferred by British shipwrights.
Coaming; is the raised edge around a hatchway or other deck openings.
Companion; a raised deck structure or shelter covering the stairway, or companion-way, leading below deck.
Counter; is the overhanging stern of a vessel.
Courses; are the square sails set from the lower yards of a square rigged vessel. Named as the fore-course, main-course, and mizzen-course; alternatively they are called the fore-sail, main-sail, and crossjack.
Cringle; is the eye in a sail boltrope.
Cross a yard; is to secure a yard to the mast with parrel or truss.
Crossjack-yard; is the lower yard of the mizzen mast. It is also a term used in fore and aft rigged vessels for the yard below the lower crosstrees for setting a running square sail, also called a crossjack sail.
Crosstrees; are wood or iron structures arranged athwarships, which together with trestletrees and cheeks, support the lower masthead assembly. See Figure 28 "Crosstrees". This is a collective term for the masthead assembly, or the doublings, in fore and aft rigged vessels with two part masts. It is also used for the masthead assembly between topmast and topgallant masts of three part masts in square riggged vessels.
Crutch; is the structure or chock on which the boom of a gaff sail rests.
Cuddy; is a small cabin in a vessels bow.
Cutwater; is the part of the vessels stem which meets the water.
Deadeyes; circular wooden blocks with three holes, through which the lanyards pass to the chainplates, for securing the shrouds and backstays.
Deadrise; is the angle the vessels bottom makes with the keel or from the horizontal.
Depth of a vessel is the vertical distance from gunwhale to keel.
Displacement; the mass of water displaced by a floating vessel. Displacement tonnage is the actual weight of the vessel, used for naval vessels.
Dolphin striker; another term for martingale boom.

Doubling; is the masthead assembly, between lower masts, topmasts and topgallant masts.
Downhauls; are lines used to haul down, jibs, and staysails during furling.
Drag; the amount by which a vessel floats lower at the after end compared to the forward end.
Draft; or lines, is a drawing showing the construction of a vessel.
Draught; (draft), the vertical distance between the waterline and the lowest part of the hull. Read off markings on the stem and stern.
Double topsails and double topgallants; formed by dividing one large sail into two, to produce lower and upper topsails and lower and upper topgallants.
Driver; is the alternative name for the spanker, or the aftermost gaff sail of a full rigged ship or barque.
Ensign staff; the pole on the taffrail which hoists the ensign flag.
Entry; the forward underwater part of a vessel.
Eyebolts; are deck fixtures, screws or bolts with circular heads, connecting with shackle hooks, purchases or rigging.
Fairlead; a fixture, guiding a rope in a desired direction.
Fall; the running end of a tackle or purchase on which the crew or winches haul.
Fashion pieces; are timbers used to form the shape of the stern.
Fid; is a piece of wood or iron, forming part of the masthead assembly. It passes through the upper mast heel and rests on the trestletreees.
Fiddle head; is a carving at the vessels stem head shaped inwardly.
Fife rail; is around the foot of the mast for belaying pins.
Figurehead; is the carving above the cutwater at the stem head.
Flemish horse; the outer part of the footrope (horse), near the yardarm.
Floor; the lowest timber portion of a frame. See frame.
Flying jib; is the outermost jib or headsail.
Foot-ropes; is the rope below the yard or bowsprit for crewmen to stand on. Also the boltrope on the lower edge of a sail.
Fore and aft sails; staysails, gaffsails, lugsails, and gaff topsails.
Forebitter; a song sung off duty, not a working song or chanty.
Forefoot; part where stempost connects with keel.
Foremast; is the mast nearest the bow in a vessel with more than one mast. If the second mast is smaller – it is called the mainmast – as in a ketch, or "one-and-a half mast" vessels.
Foresail; a loosley used term for the:

1. Forecourse of square rigged vessels;
2. Forestay sail in cutters, dandy smacks and ketches;
3. Gaff fore sail in schooners.

Forestay; a strong wire from the foremast hounds to the stem head, provides mast and sail support.
Frame; is composed of timbers named; floor, futtock and top timber, which also form a rib.
Freeboard; the vertical distance from the upper deck level to the waterline.
Furl; when a sail is folded, or rolled, up on its yard, stay, or boom, and bound with gaskets.
Futtock (foothook); one of the timbers forming a frame or rib.
Futtock shrouds; are the stays from the mast to the rim of the top, or the "crosstrees".
Gaff, or gaff spar; is the spar along the head of a fore and aft sail.
Gaff jaws; together with the parrel, connect the gaff spar to the mast. A standing gaff stays aloft. A hoisting gaff is raised and lowered.
Gaff-sail; is the foursided, fore and aft, sail, bent to the gaff spar. Named as; gaff foresail, gaff mainsail, and gaff mizzen sail. In general usage these terms are reduced to; foresail, mainsail, and mizzen sail. The latter gaff mizzen sail is also called a spanker, driver, or trysail.
Gaff topsail; a sail set above the gaff. The foot of the gaff topsail is spread along the gaff spar.
Gallant, or garland; term applied to masts, sails, tops and stays.
Gallery; the stern balcony in galleons and men-of-war.
Gammoning; a lashing used in bowsprits.
Garboard; is the hull strake next to the keel.
Gaskets; short ropes for securing the sail to the yard or boom during furling.
Gear; a term for rigging, tackle ropes or lines, used in all shipboard working equipment.
Gin block; is an alternative name for the tye block
Gipsy; the sprocketed cable holder of a windlass.
Ground tackle; anchors, cables and mooring gear.
Gudgeons; are brackets with an eye, fixed to the sternpost, to take the rudder pintles.
Gun tackle is composed of rope roved through two single blocks.
Gunwale; the upper rail, or strake, covering the inner sides of a wooden boat. It strengthens the boats frame heads and helps to provide sheer.
Guy; a rope to steady a spar, such as a boom.
Gyn or gin; tackle is composed of rope roved through two blocks; a double and a treble block.
Half deck; is the poop deck aft above the upper deck.
Halyard, haulyard; lines or ropes to hoist and lower the yards, sails,

and flags.
Hanks; are the hooks or rings connecting the staysail to the stays.
Hatch, or hatchway; is a deck opening into the cargo hold.
Hawse pipes; or hawse holes, are iron leads in the bow through which the anchor cables pass.
Headgear; the rigging at the vessels stem, bowsprit and jibboom.
Headsails; a general term for the forestay sails and jib sails.
Heel; is the lower part of a mast or bowsprit.
Hoisting yards are the following; single topsail, single topgallant, upper topsail, upper topgallant and royal yards, they are lowered or hoisted during furling and setting sails.
Hoops; are wooden or metal rings connecting the luff of a fore-and-aft sail to a mast.
Horse; is a name for the yard or bowsprit footrope, sheet tackle connects with an athwartship horse in fore-and-aft rigged vessels.
Hounds; are the flattened parts, or projections, of the mast below the masthead, forming the top and "crosstrees".
Hull; is the vessels body.
Inhaul; draw in a spar or sail.
Inwale; is a stiffening of the upper strake inwards of the gunwale.
Jackstaff; a flag pole at the bow or stem head. Developed from the spritsail topsail mast.
Jackstay; is either a rope or iron rod fixed parallel to a yard to which the sail is bent.
Jackyard topsail; set above the gaff mainsail, it has a wooden spar laced along its luff and foot, called the jackyard.
Jacobs ladder; is a rope ladder with wooden steps.
Jaws; are the ends of a gaff spar, or boom, connecting with the mast.
Jeers; are the tackle used to hoist or lower the lower yards.
Jib; is a a triangular staysail set on a headstay.
Jib-boom; is an extension of the bowsprit.
Jib-headed gaff topsail; is the triangular topsail above the gaff mainsail.
Jigger mast; is the after mast on a four masted vessel.
Jury; means temporary – jury rig, jury rudder, jury mast or jury steering gear.
Keel; the central longitudinal timber forming the backbone of a vessels framework
Keelson; or hog, is fitted above the keel and floors to provide extra strength.
Knee; a supporting rectangular bracket.
Knee of the head; is that part of the stem supporting the figurehead.
Knightheads; are strong timbers on either side of the stem fixing

the end of the bowsprit in position. They also function as bollard timbers, or bitts, for the anchor cable.
Knot; is the speed of a vessel in nautical miles per hour.
Lacing; the rope connecting staysail to the stay, or the gaff sail to the gaff spar and boom. The rope is passed through eyes in the sail, or laced.
Lanyards; short lengths of rope in the deadeyes for tightening the shrouds or backstays.
Lapstrake; alternative name for clinker built hull.
Lateen sail; a triangular shaped sail with its luff bent to a lateen yard.
Legs; are timbers fitted outside the vessel to keep her upright when dried out at low water.
Leech; or leach, are the sail side edges.
Length; is either over all between perpendiculars from stem to stern, or on the water line.
Lift; is a tackle or rope, which support, trim, or top up, the yard; extending from yardarms to the mast head.
Lines; a general term for ropes.
Lizard; a short rope or wire with an eye or thimble at one end, it acts as a fairlead for headsail downhauls.
Loose footed; is a gaff sail without a boom.
Lubbers hole; the opening in the deck of a lower masthead top, an alternative way to reach the top than by the futtock shrouds.
Luff; is the leading edge, or forward leech, of a fore and aft sail.
Lugsail; is a fore and aft, foursided sail, having a wider throat than a gaffsail. Types include dipping lugsail and standing lugsail all of which are bent to a lug yard. The lug yard hangs obliquely to the mast.
Lying to, or to try, or to heave to; when a vessel is stopped under reduced canvas during heavy stormy weather.
Main mast; is the principal mast in a single masted vessel, and the second mast from the bow in all other vessels except the 'one and a half masted' vessels, ketches, galliots, dandy smacks, flats and yawls where it is the first mast from the bow.
Martingale; or dolphin striker is the short perpendicular spar below the bowsprit.
Martingale; stays lead downwards from the jib-boom end to the martingale or dolphin striker spar thus staying the jib-boom.
Mast coat; a canvas cover around the mast at deck level.
Mast hole; circular hole in the deck through which the mast passes.
Mast hoops; are wooden rings which connect luff of a gaffsail to the mast.
Mast parts; are named as follows;the lower mast or the first mast

part from the deck; the topmast is the second mast part from the deck; the topgallant mast is the third mast part from the deck; the royal mast is the fourth mast part from the deck.
Mast partners; are mast supports in the deck framing.
Mast-step; the part into which the mast heel, is located and fixed.
Mast wedges; are driven around the mast at deck level, to provide support.
Merchant Shipping Acts; prior to 1660 were called Navigation Acts.
Mizzen, mizen; is the third mast from the bow, or the smaller mast in "one and a half masted vessels", ketches etc.
Mould; a wooden transverse framework or pattern, used in boat construction to obtain the boats shape.
Multi-masted vessels have masts named in the following order from the bow: foremast, mainmast, mizzen mast, jigger mast, spanker mast, driver mast and pusher mast; alternatively they are called: foremast, mainmast, mizzen mast, No. 4 mast, No. 5 mast, No. 6 mast and spanker mast.
Oakum; untwisted old rope used for caulking.
Orlop deck; is the lowest deck in a vessel. The deck immediately above it is called the lower deck.
Outhaul; a line or rope to haul a sail outboard along a spar.
Outrigger; or small bumpkin; a projecting spar for a sail.
Painter; is a rope at the stem of a boat for towing or making fast.
Parrel, parral; is a rope or iron collar on a hoisting yard, allowing the yard to rotate or be lowered or raised. Parrel beads threaded through the parrel wire or rope allow ease of movement. Early vessels had a rope parrel connected to the middle and lower part of the sail, in addition to holding the yard spar to the mast.
Parrel truck; wooden rollers, or beads, forming the gaff jaw rope.
Peak; is the upper outer end of a gaff sail, or a gaff spar. Hauled down with the peak downhaul line.
Pinrail; is a board to hold the belaying pins.
Pintle; is the part of the stern post connecting with the gudgeon of the rudder.
Plank; is either a whole strake, or part, of a strake.
Pole mast; is a mast made of one piece .
Poop; a raised after deck, or deck above the quarter deck.
Pully – hauly; the work involved in pulling and hauling in sailing vessels.
Purchase; is an arrangement of ropes and blocks for lifting and hauling purposes.
Pusher; is the name given to the seventh mast from the bow in a multimasted vessel.

Quarter; the after parts of the vessels side.
Quarter deck; is the part of the deck abaft of the mainmast.
Rabbet; the groove in the keel to receive the garboard strake.
Rake; is the inclination angle formed by the mast.
Rails; an alternative term for bulwarks.
Ratlines; short ropes between the shrouds, which form a ladder to go aloft.
Reef; is to reduce the sail area by rolling it up or tying it to its boom or yard. Reef points or short lengths of rope are used to tie up the rolled up sail.
Reeve; or rove, is the act of passing a rope through an opening of a pulley block.
Rib; is a timber composed of a single frame. See frame.
Rig; is the arrangement of masts, spars and sails of a sailing vessel-fore-and-aft rig and square rig.
Rigging is the gear, ropes, wires, tackle needed to work a vessel, to support masts, move yards, spars and sails; consists of standing and running rigging.
Rim; is the outer edge of the masthead assembly top.
Roach; is the deep curvature in the foot of a square sail, or in a gaff topsail.
Robands; rope bands, or rovings, lengths of plaited yarn for bending sails to the yard or gaff spar.
Rowlock; is a crutch on the gunwale supporting an oar.
Royal; is the mast or sail above the topgallant, or yard connecting with the sail.
Rubbing strake or piece; also called outer wale, fitted beneath the gunwale, protects vessel side from chafing when alongside a quay etc.
Run; is the underwater after part part of a hull.
Running; means loose or movable, or not fixed.
Running rigging; is the system of sail or gear handling ropes which operate through blocks.
Running square-sail; is a square sail set on the foremast foreyard, spreader yard, or crossjack, of a fore and aft vessel, sloop, cuttter, or schooner when running before the wind. It is a temporary fine weather sail.
Sails; are of two main kinds; square sails bent to a yard athwartships; and fore-and-aft sails set on a stays, gaff spar or boom in a lengthwise direction.
Samson or king post; a very strong bollard or post for anchor and mooring cables.
Scuppers; are holes in the bulwarks or waterways, fitted with wash ports, flaps or doors, to allow deckwater to flow outboard.

Scuttle; a small deck opening covered by a sliding or lifting top. Also the name for portholes or openings in a vessels hull sides.
Scroll heads; are stemhead carvings curving outwards.
Seams; are the spaces between planks caulked with oakum and payed with pitch tar.
Seize; is to fasten two ropes together.
Serve; is to cover up or bind something; e.g. a rope with canvas or line.
Set-flying, a sail set without a stay, spar, hanks or a yard, it has a sheet, halyard and tack; e.g. flying jib sail of a sloop.
Set-standing; a sail which is set on a stay or spar, attached by hanks which prevent the sail flying in the wind, e.g. cutter fore staysail.
Set sail; is to haul up and loosen sails or to make sail.
Shanty, or chanty; is a shipboard work song accompaniment for hauling or heaving on ropes. Forebitter is not.
Sheathing; a protective covering of copper metal against ship worm applied to the underwater part of a hull.
Sheer line; or sheer, is the upper edge of a hull. It is the upward curve of the deck seen in the bow.
Sheerpole; is fitted horizontally at the bottom of the shrouds.
Sheer strake; is the highest strake in the planking of a boat.
Sheets; are lines, chains, or ropes connected to a sails lowest corner.
Shrouds; are mast supporting ropes connected to the masthead and a vessels sides, they are part of the standing rigging system.
Skylight; a glazed deck opening admitting light and air into a cabin below.
Sling; is the chain supporting the centre of a lower yard.
Slings; is a term describing the centre of a yard.
Skysails; are sails set above the royal sails in fair weather.
Snotter; a rope loop or metal ring holding the heel of a sprit or gaff spar to the mast.
Snowmast, or trysail mast; connects with the trysail luff by way of hoops.
Spars; are wooden sail and rigging supports, eg, masts, yards, gaffs, booms, sprits and jackyards.
Spanker; or driver, is a name for the fore-and-aft sail, with a boom and gaff, on the aftermost mast of a barque.
Spencer; is a type of gaffsail, or fore and aft sail, set on any mast other than the aftermost mast of a full rigged ship. It is usually without a boom or loose footed.
Spider band; is around the lower part of a mast fitted with belaying pins.
Spritsail; is a fore and aft sail extended diagonally by a sprit spar.
Spritsails; or bowsprit sails, were the foursided sails located below

the bowsprit in early carracks, galleons, men of war and merchantmen.
Squaresails; foursided sails which are bent to a yard.
Standing jib; a name for the inner jib sail, set from the bowsprit, or stem head.
Stanchions; are upright structures supporting the bulwarks or rails.
Standing; means a fixed structure.
Standing rigging; is that system of rigging, which supports masts and spars, and is not moved, or is fixed.
Standing yards; are fixed to the mast and include the lower course yards, lower topsail and lower topgallant yards.
Staysails; are bent on the stays.
Stays; are mast supporting ropes connected to the masthead in a fore and aft direction.
Storm sails; a trysail or storm jib, made of heavy canvas.
Steeve; or steeving, is the angle the bowsprit makes with the horizontal or horizon line.
Stem; is the main framework timber in a vessels bow. It is often strengthened with an apron, knee and deadwood.
Step; of a mast is the part into which the mast heel fits.
Sternpost; is the main framework timber in a vessels stern. A stern knee and deadwood strengthens the sternpost.
Stirrups; connect the footrope to the yard.
Strake; is a continuous plank made of one or more pieces, extending from stem to stern.
Studding sails; are light foursided sails, set outside the square sails, which can be set in fair weather when running before the wind.
Stringer; is a longitudinal support, situated inside the hull planking.
Swigging or sweating; is the tightening of the halyards by giving them an extra pull.
Tack; is the lower forward corner of a fore and aft sail.
Tackle; is a purchase made with a rope passing through two blocks.
Taffrail; is the rail around the stern.
Thimble; a metal ring or eye with an incurving side allowing a rope to be spliced around it.
Thole; is a wooden pin on the gunwale connecting with the grommet of an oar.
Throat; is the inner top corner of a gaffsail.
Thwart; is the transverse, athwartships, seat in a wooden boat.
Tiller; is a bar in the rudder head to steer with.
Timbers; a name for the ribs or frames, connecting with the keel,providing strength and form to a vessel hull; see frame. Also a loose term for any large sized pieces of wood used in vessel

construction.

Tonnage; *Gross tonnage* is a measure of a vessels cargo carrying capacity, including accommodation and other spaces.

Net tonnage is a measure of the vessels cargo carrying capacity alone and excludes accommodation and other spaces.

Top; is the lower mast head assembly, in a three part mast. Found in all fully square rigged vessels; full rigged ships, barques, brigs, brigantines and barquentines. Tops are composed of: crosstrees, trestletrees, deck planking and rims, all supported by the hounds and cheeks. See Figure 48.

Tops are not present in schooners, sloops, smacks, and other vessels with two part masts.

Additional tops were present between the topmast and topgallant mast in galleons, ships of the line and early merchantmen, and were called upper tops. Also found in brigs.

Topgallant mast; is the mast above the topmast.

Topmast; is the mast above the lower mast.

Topping lift; is a rope to lift the end of a swinging spar or boom.

Topsails; are the sails above the courses in square rigged vessels, or above the running square sail foreyard in schooners, and other fore-and-aft rigged vessels.

Top timbers; are the highest timbers, above the futtock timbers, in a vessels frame or rib.

Transom; the athwartship structure fixed to the sternpost forming a vessel's stern.

Traveller; is an iron ring which slides along a bowsprit, stay or the horse-that rod to which the sheets of sails connect. The ring which slides up and down a lugsail mast.

Treenail; is a wooden peglike through fastening used in planking.

Trestletrees; are the fore and aft arranged horizontal structures which support the crosstrees in the masthead assembly. The fid rests on the trestletrees.

Transom; the athwartship structure, fixed to the sternpost, which forms a vessels stern.

Truck; is the top piece of a mast. It can be disc or spherical in shape.

Truss; is the gear which holds a fixed yard to the mast, and allows only vertical and horizontal movement.

Try; is to heave to, or lie under storm canvas, reduced sail, or bare poles, during stormy weather.

Trysail; or storm sail, is a small strong threesided sail used in bad weather instead of the foursided gaff sail. An alternative name for a barques spencer, and spanker of a brig or snow. It is also called a jibheaded gaff sail.

Tumblehome; is the inward slope of a vessels side.

Tun; a large wine cask holding 252 gallons, or 1135 litres.
Tunnage; a tax on every tun of wine.
Tye; a chain shackled to the yard slings, which is connected to the hoisting yard halliard. See Figure 59.
Tye block, or tie block, also called gin block; is part of the yard halliard system. It is a fixed, or standing, single metal block.
Unfurl; cast off the sail gaskets to set sail.
Upper deck; the highest continuous deck.
Vangs; are ropes which steady the gaff or sprit spars ends.
Vessel; any kind of watercraft.
Votive ship; a model of a vessel placed in a church.
Waist; part of the vessel upper deck forward of the quarter deck, or poop, or between the fore and main masts.
Waterway; a raised deck timber fitted below the bulwarks guiding water to drain out of the scupper drain holes.
Wale; is a strake thicker than the others, running longitudinally to protect the hull – also called a rubbing strake.
Warp; is a light strong rope or wire.
Weigh; to lift the anchor to allow the vessel to get under weigh.
Whelps; ribs on the capstan, winch and windlass barrels to grip the cables or warps.
Winch; is a machine for hauling on ropes. Used partly for cargo handling.
Windlass; is a machine for raising and lowering the anchor. It is horizontal in comparison to the vertical capstan. It is used mainly in merchant vessels.
Woolding; is the act of winding a rope around a made-mast or spar.
Yardarms; are the ends of a yard.
Yards; are the spars on which square sails, lateen sails, gaff topsails, and lugsails are set. Square sail yards are of two main types:
a) fixed or standing yards connect with the mast by bands, trusses and cranes. Fixed yards have the following square sails bent to them: courses, lower topsails and lower topgallant sails.
b) movable or hoisting yards connect with the mast through sliding parrals. Hoisting yards have the following square sails bent to them: single topsail, single topgallant, royals, upper topsails and upper topgallants.
Yards ropes; and staysail holyards connect the running square sail to the foreyard.

BIBLIOGRAPHY

David Thomas; *Hen Longau Sir Gaernarfon* and *Hen Longau a Llongwyr Cymru.*

Institute of Welsh Maritime Historical Studies, MOROL, book series since 2005.

Cymru a'r Môr/Maritime Wales Gwynedd Archives, annually since 1975.

Sea Breezes, monthly since 1919.

Ships in Focus Record quarterly since 1996.

Ships Monthly, since 1986

National Maritime Museum, Greenwich; *Catalogue of historic photographs, Vol 2; Merchant Sailing Ships.*

Bass, George F.; *A history of seafaring*

Bennet, Douglas; *Schooner Sunset*

Binns, Alan; *Viking voyages.*

Coppack, Tom; *A lifetime with ships.*

Cottter Jim; *Soren Larsen-homeward round the Horn.*

Chambers-Jones R.; *Sailing the Strait.*

Chapelle Howard I.; *History of American sailing ships.*

Campbell-Jones Susan; *Welsh sail.*

Davies, John Ifor; *Growing up among sailors; Sŵn y môr.*

Davies, J. Glyn; *Cerddi Edern; Cherddi Porth Dinllaen.*

Davies, J. H.; *Blas y môr.*

Davis, Charles G.; *Ship model builders assistant.*

Dudszus Alfred and Henriot Ernest; *Dictionary of Ship Types.*

Eames, Aled; *Ships and seamen of Anglesey; Porthmadog Ships; Meistri moroedd; Shipmaster; Twilight of Welsh Sail; Gwraig y capten; Ventures in sail; Pobl môr y Port; Y fordaith bell; Shrouded quays, O Bwllheli i ben draw y byd*

Ellis, H. Rees; *Rhwng môr a mynydd*

England, Richard; *Schoonerman.*

Fishlock, Trevor; *Fishlocks sea stories*

Francis, Dewi; *Master Mariner – Capt Wm. H. Hughes, DSC.*

Greenhill, Basil; *Evolution of the wooden ship; The life and death of the merchant sailing ship – The Ship 7 – 1815-1965.*

Griffith, David; *Morwyr Cymru (Traethawd Eisteddfod Genedlaethol Caerlleon 1866)*

Griffith, John, *Llythyrau hen forwr.*
Gruffydd, Elfed; *Ar hyd ben 'rallt.*
Hope, Bryan D.; *A commodious yard.*
Hope, Ronald; *History of British shipping.*
Hughes, Beti; *O sŵn y don.*
Hughes, Henry; *Immortal sails, Through mighty seas.*
Hugill, Stan; *Shanties and sailors songs.*
Hurst, Alex A.; *Square-riggers the final epoch; The medley of mast and sail 1 and 2.*
Huws, Gwyn Pari; *Y Fenai.*
Jenkins, J. Geraint; *Traddodiad y môr; Welsh sailing ships and sailing men, Inshore fishermen of Wales, The coracle.*
Jones, Evan; *Yr hogyn llongau hwyliau.*
Jones, Geraint and Williams, Dafydd; *Trefor.*
Jones, Gwilym; *Wedi'r llanw.*
Jones, Ivor Wynne; *Welsh shipwrecks.*
Jones, Joseph Seth; *Dyddiadur y Mimosa.*
Jones-Morris, John, L.; *Eifionydd a'r môr.*
Jones-Williams, John; *Y llongwr o Ros-Lan.*
Kemp, Peter; *Oxford companion to ships and the sea.*
Landstrom, Bjorn; *The ship.*
Lewis, E. A.; *The Welsh port books 1550-1603.*
Lewis, M. J. T.; *Sails on the Dwyryd.*
Lloyd Jones, R.; *Capten; Atgofion hen forwr; Mate y Mona; Ynys y trysor.*
Lloyd, Lewis; *The brig Susannah of Aberdyfi, Unity of Barmouth, The port of Caernarfon.*
Lloyd Hughes, D. G., *Hanes tref Pwllheli.*
Lloyd, L. J., *The Lancashire Nobby.*
Lubbock, Basil; *Round the Horn before the mast; Last of the windjammers 1 and 2.*
March, Edgar J.; *Inshore craft of Britain 1 & 2.*
McGrail, Sean; *Rafts, boats and ships – The Ship 1 – Prehistoric to Medieval.*
McGowan, Alan, *Tiller and whipstaff – The Ship 3 – 1470-1700; The century before steam – The Ship 4 – 1700-1820.*
MacGregor, David R.; *The schooner.*
Owen, Gwilym; *Pentref Trefor a chwarel yr Eifl.*
Owen, Hugh; *Treasures of the Mawddach.*
Parry, Henry; *Wreck and rescue on the coasts of of Wales 1 and 2.*

Richards, John, *Maritime Wales.*
Roberts, Ellis, *Ar frig y don.*
Roberts, H. & Nolan, M.; *Porthmadog ships – The Newfoundland fish boxes.*
Roberts. Owain T.P., et al, *Inshore Craft – Traditional Working Vessels British Isles.*
Roberts, R. J.; *Ar y môr.*
Rowland, William; *Y llong lo;*
Senior, Michael; *Did Prince Madog discover America.*
Severin, Tim; *Brendan voyage.*
Shewin, Andrew; *Great days of sail.*
Simper, R.; *Britains Maritime Heritage; Gaff Sail.*
Smyth, W. H.; *The sailors word-book 1867.*
Smyle, Mike; *Herring fishers of Wales.*
Spurling, J.; *Sail – The romance of the clipper ships.*
Stammers, M. K.; *West coast shipping; Discovering maritime museums. Mersey flats and flatsmen; A maritime fortress – Belan, The passage makers; Claytons annual register of shipping and ports.*
Time Life Books; *The windjammers; The Vikings; The pirates; The clipper ships; The Pacific navigators; The explorers* and *Liverpool Sailing Ships.*
Underhill, Harold A.; *Sailing ships rigs and rigging, Deepwater sail.*
Villiers, Alan; *The way of a ship.*
Williams, E. Roland; *Elizabethan Wales.*
Williams, Dafydd and Jones, Geraint; *Trefor.*
Williams, D.J.; *Anturiaethau Morwyr Cymru.*
White, E. W.; *British fishing-boats and coastal craft 1 &2.*
Williams, Elis; *Packet to Ireland, Bangor port of Beaumaris.*
Williams, J. G.; *Pigau'r sêr.*
Williams, W. E.; *Llyncu'r angor; Ar y bont; O flaen y mast, Hwylio'r moroedd.*

* * * *

Videos:
Mynd fel pawb i forio – Ffilmiau Nant, Caernarfon. *Soren Larsen* voyage.
Around Cape Horn; Mystic Seaport – distributors – Beckmann, West St, Ramsey, Isle Of Man.
Last sailors; DDVideos, Churchill Court, N. Harrow, HA2 75A.
The age of sail; DDVideos, Churchill Court, N. Harrow, HA2 75A.

AUTHOR BIOGRAPHICAL

Fred Kilgour a chartered biologist, educator, and established author. He was born at Penygroes, Caernarfonshire, and comes from a Liverpool seafaring family, was partly reared in his early years at Croeshigol, Trefor, and was educated at Pwllheli and the Liverpool College of Technology and London University.

From a very early age he has messed about in boats on the beaches of Llŷn, and in the Mersey docklands from where he made coasting voyages in his father's tramp ships; thus starting a lifetimes enthusiasm for all things maritime. Sailing in a nobby, drifter, trawler, Scottish puffer, brig, brigantine, barque; and in his own open fishing boat; an experience gained in between being a Technical College senior science lecturer, examiner, Seafarers Education Service tutor, and in writing many textbooks on natural and applied science.

He is a keen ship modeller, stimulated by the experience of watching, and in mainly backing up the roving iron for local quarrymen and carpenters building clinker boats in Trefor.

A founder member of the Jubilee Sailing Trust – providing offshore sailing experience in square rigged sailing vessels for disabled people. Abroad he has successfully supported and investigated offshore sailing for disabled people in New Zealand, and West Australia, and believes fervently in establishing a sail training ship for the people of Wales as in other maritime nations.

A fluent Welsh speaker, and occasional contributor to *Llafar Gwlad*, an activity which he regards as his essential formal education in Welsh.

He lives in sight of the sea in Old Colwyn and gets afloat in his small boat off Trefor.